On Pilgrimage

On Pilgrimage

☙❧

Douglas C. Vest

COWLEY PUBLICATIONS
Cambridge ✦ Boston
Massachusetts

Published in the United States of America by Cowley Publications, a division of the Society of St. John the Evangelist. No portion of this book may be reproduced, stored in or introduced into a retrieval system, or transmitted, in any form or by any means—including photocopying—without the prior written permission of Cowley Publications, except in the case of brief quotations embodied in critical articles and reviews.

Library of Congress Cataloging-in-Publication Data:
Vest, Douglas C.
    On pilgrimage / Douglas C. Vest
        p.   cm.
    Includes bibliographical references.
    ISBN 1-56101-150-9 (alk. paper)
    1. Christian pilgrims and pilgrimages. 2. Vest, Douglas C. I. Title.
BX2320.V37   1998
263'.041—dc21   97-47374

Cynthia Shattuck, editor; Vicki Black, copyeditor and designer
Cover art from a photograph taken in the Devon countryside.

This book is printed on recycled, acid-free paper and was produced in the United States of America.

Cowley Publications   •   28 Temple Place
Boston, Massachusetts 02111
800-225-1534   •   http://www.cowley.org/~cowley

Several sages over the centuries have written that the real point of traveling is not to arrive but to return home. How thankful I am to have been at home—wherever we were together—with Alice, Jim and Nancy and their Joshua and Anna; Christine and Don; and Norvene! As we have shared so much of our lives, I trust that they will gladly share dedication of a pilgrimage through these printed pages with the scores of fellow travelers who have accompanied me to sites that bond me to my spiritual forebears in Great Britain.

Contents

A Note from the Author

As a practical comment for your consideration, I
suggest that the following chapters be viewed as
themselves a pilgrim's path: reading done in a
reflective manner, not rushing through successive
chapters but giving time to reflect what the writing is
conveying at the moment of reading. Suggested
exercises to aid individual or group reflection are
appended to each chapter. I wish you pleasant
journeying through the pages.

Chapter One

A Homecoming Away from Home

Something to bring back to show
you have been there: a lock of God's
hair, stolen from him while he was
asleep, a photograph of the garden
of the spirit. As has been said,
the point of travelling is not
to *arrive* but to *return home*
laden with pollen you shall work up
into honey the mind feeds on.

R. S. Thomas

Periodically I feel an urge to travel somewhere, well away from familiar settings. Ordinarily these occasions are not a response to crises, for which I am grateful, nor are they for business reasons. Is wanderlust at the root of my mild unrest? Probably not, because my desire is not simply to be away from home and on the road, but to visit a particular place. Am I seeking escape, or to reconnect with something important in my past but now absent? Maybe so, but there are at least three other contributing factors, each one common to all of us.

First, we human beings are born possessing an innate motility. We want to move, to express our mobility, and being able to move calls forth the energy required to do so. Toward what shall we move? A second element comes into play shortly after our birth, probably as soon as we become aware that there is something out there beyond ourselves. We think, "How much of me is part of 'out there'? I'd better go see!"

A baby's first steps are thrilling—for the parents if not for the unsteady, tottering infant—and exploration takes several forms. Newborns of many other species quickly learn to forage for food. Although today's human babies are not without appetites, their more dramatic movements seem a succession of efforts to leave the crib, then the playpen, next the yard, and into the neighborhood and beyond. Maybe these are acts to assert our individuality as well as follow our curiosity, but they are also fueled by our need to keep testing our ability to move. An infant cannot explain his sense that "there's something out there—more to the world than what I can see," but he can move!

Alongside these two inborn tendencies is a third element: attachment to home, the place where security and identity are found. I imagine that these three elements of motility, curiosity, and attachment to a place require a full lifetime to work out in order to achieve a sense of peace. St. Augustine related this search for a sense of peace to the search for God when he wrote in his *Confessions,* "You have made us for yourself, O Lord, and our heart is restless until we find our rest in you." We are born for relationship with the transcendent, and we are restless until we satisfy this longing for closer union with God.

I imagine that a similar restlessness arises from another source. To paraphrase and personalize Augustine's conviction: "You have placed us in an enchanting and awesome creation, O Lord, and our hearts are restless until we have explored the Earth, with which we share life." We are invited to relate to the transcendent in our mobile flesh as well as in our restless spirits. Augustine's phrase "we find our rest *in you*" is in Latin *ad te*, which I prefer to translate *toward you*. Our disquiet finds its release throughout life not so much through assurance of positive outcomes, but by our constantly turning toward God. In a similar way, our response to the universe is to turn increasingly outward toward creation rather than merely to our own *inner resources*. That necessarily involves movement as we seek to broaden and deepen our acquaintance with the world around us.

So we human beings experience two strong pulls: to remain in our secure homes among special relationships, but also to venture away from home. What makes us leave home for an extended period of time? I call it the "pilgrim impulse," which bids us forth not only in curiosity, but also in the conviction that the journey offers fulfillment of our longings. Pilgrimage is primarily journey to a place which promises adventure, new options, change, and renewal. The journey may bestow more than those elements, but here I am talking about a level of self-assurance that grows into a yearning to investigate for oneself beyond the security of home.

People have gone on pilgrimage for millennia, long before the ancient journey of Abraham and Sarah, and extending into our own times. Some places are considered special because God seems more accessible there, and are visited by millions of people each year.

Other places are meaningful for personal reasons, but both kinds evoke expectations sufficient to energize our journeys, which at times can be arduous and prolonged. Both can be called sacred journeys, a good alternate name for pilgrimage.

Though God's call to Abraham and Sarah can be interpreted as a brief, dramatic invitation, I am also convinced that sustained yearning is an important element of pilgrimage. Some possibility dwells within us until, finally, one day the determination to begin our journey comes gently but surely, and that is when we decide to venture forth on pilgrimage.

Unlike sightseeing or business travel, pilgrimage has an avowed spiritual dimension. Our society, if not characterized by spiritual awakening, at least exhibits a grasping for the spiritual. Ironically, this comes at a time when no one can agree whether interest in organized religion is growing or waning. The central acts of a religious tradition are repeatedly "celebrated," a word rooted in the Latin for "much frequented." But repetition can be viewed as overly routine, if not boring, by a society deluged by constant and varied entertainment. It is certainly true that in the midst of competing claims on their time and energy, for many people formal worship is relegated to a leisure-time activity. "Religion doesn't do anything for me" is heard from people whose firsthand efforts range from virtually none to deep and continued seeking. The latter sort are more likely to explore spiritual paths.

The path of pilgrimage offers new settings that can stimulate us, make us more alert and open to wonder, fascination, and awe. Thus pilgrimage consists of more than a physical movement away from home to new surroundings, for it is an inward journey as well as an outward journey, into the self as well as to new places. A helpful image for me is that of pilgrims needing bifocal vision, so that they can look at objects and places from far off as well as close up. Pilgrimage consists of both a visit to a place and a meditative consideration within oneself. Thus a pilgrim's exploration of movement is not a distraction from the spiritual quest, but the quest itself.

My own explorations over a range of pilgrim experiences continue to teach me about the interactions of "out there" and "in here." In recent years, few lessons have impressed me more than the power of true presence to what is before me: the awareness of enjoying loveliness while I am enjoying it. I have become aware that my silence at a holy shrine is not because I have ceased to look for new details, but comes from a feeling of reverence. I am willling simply to be a pilgrim.

I first began to learn what it means to be a pilgrim a few years ago, halfway through a twelve-day trip wandering in Great Britain, when I realized that my long-anticipated journey was passing more quickly than I would have wished. I wondered if I could slow down the passage of time without impairing the sense of freedom that my first week had brought. In my pocket was a British Rail pass, an open two-week railway ticket purchased before leaving home. That pass constituted most of my advance planning for the trip, except for reserving a room at the beginning and a commitment to visit friends in Cornwall at the end. I was surprised that time was moving so quickly, although I had not been rushing around. Maybe simple enjoyment was the villain: time escapes from a person having fun!

It was when I arrived in Durham, an ancient cathedral city in northeastern England, that I began to realize the trip had changed from easygoing sightseeing into something else. It started me wondering about trips in general, whether they are journeys, sightseeing tours, pilgrimages, group junkets, or simply aimless wanderings. Are tours so popular because they are invitingly packaged, or can a more basic explanation be found in the innate human desire to venture beyond ourselves and our normal routines and settings? Do we creatures seek to interact with more of creation? How much sightseeing arises from a desire to visit particular sites, and how much from the need to get away from familiar places where our ordinary lives go on? Are packaged tours simply our modern equivalent of medieval pilgrimages?

On the afternoon I arrived in Durham by train, I entrusted my one large piece of luggage to a locker at the railway station, and walked toward the city's center carrying in a backpack what was essential for an overnight stay. One of my essentials was a pocket-sized book of devotions that has accompanied me during ten years of hiking and other travel. That evening I read psalms and prayers from this breviary under the towering vault of Durham Cathedral, which was virtually deserted at the time for the service of evensong.

The next morning I sat alone in the Venerable Bede Chapel at the west end of the cathedral, the book unopened while I admired the intricate carvings on the walls and the shrine containing the remains of the great chronicler of England's history from the end of Roman occupation in 410 until his own death in 735. I had twice read much of Bede's writings, and wanted to start at his memorial before going to the principal shrine at the opposite end of the cathedral, that of St. Cuthbert, with whom the imposing building is identified. How right it seemed for Bede to be resting in a spacious chapel supported by many half-circle arches typical of eleventh- and twelfth-century Romanesque architecture. All was very quiet until my reverie was broken by the sound of many feet shuffling into the chapel as forty people huddled around a guide. She spoke clearly, loudly, and with the authority of one well aware of the limited time she had for a deluge of details. As the group took their seats on short benches alongside mine, I judged them to be mostly retirees from northern England. I remained in place among the group, covertly listening with my eyes on my book, now open but still unread.

The guide did not acknowledge Bede, but opened with: "St. Cuthbert's body remained incorruptible for about three hundred years, whereupon it was committed to its resting place here in this cathedral." For a moment, the guide's announcement seemed to strike the group speechless. I thought about the fact that Bishop David Jenkins of this very cathedral had recently raised questions about the factuality of Jesus' resurrection, and that many in the Church of England had seen his opinions as a great departure from orthodoxy. His questions had threatened long-held views in matters of faith, whereas our guide's talk fired the imagination. No doubt it is the guides' imaginative approaches and not theology that have attracted many of the millions who have visited the shrine of Cuthbert over the passage of ten centuries.

Later, over a pot of tea in the cathedral lunch room, I began to question my reasons for being here. Was I on a casual trip to sites I had long heard about, or on a pilgrimage that might reveal something deeper about my expectations? What was motivating me, arousing my curiosity with new information, and sustaining me in motion? Had pure recreation become mixed with something else that would remain after I went home? Why was I on this trip, and why did I choose to take this trip alone?

Several reasons converged in my mind, some devotional and some recreational. The devotional element arose from a desire to enrich my life as a Benedictine oblate, someone who is attracted to monastic principles and living under a modified vow, married and "in the world"—in my case, sixty miles away from the monastery to which I felt closely bonded. Taking time off after a year of intensive work was also in the picture; this wandering trip began the morning after two weeks of leading two dozen people on an exploration of Benedictine traditions and settings. I was alone because my wife needed to return to our home three weeks before me, and I enjoy being on my own to explore unfamiliar sites. Still another element was my persistent curiosity about what it would have been like to live in or near a monastery several centuries ago—something better learned from personal encounter than from books. In any case, I sensed that I was in the middle of an important experiment.

Still thinking about this, I entered the small gift shop housed within the complex of structures bordering the south side of the cathedral where the monks had lived centuries earlier. My progress through the shop was slow, however, because a virtual crush of sightseers had come to buy something before two chartered coaches waiting outside would carry them off to their next destination. Their haste and need to buy was contagious: I began to feel the same pressure to choose something for my wife. From the racks of postcards, tea towels, key chains, rosary beads, jewelry, books, and other items that I never even reached, I found some earrings of an interwoven Celtic design. But why was I in such a hurry? Not only did I have no reason to rush, I had in fact added to the crush and confusion in the shop. I had been just as impatient to make my purchases as those on tightly programmed schedules. Somehow I had been caught up in the frenzy within a tiny room of a massive building. Moreover, my second purchase was exactly what many other tourists had bought: a booklet about the cathedral's structure and history, and picture cards of the stout Norman architecture much clearer than I could obtain from my camera. The booklet would guide me through the cathedral while I was still inundated by sights and facts, and later on the cards would serve as proof to others that I had actually beheld the massive structure of Durham Cathedral.

The feelings of irritation and petty criticism that surfaced while I was crowded into the cathedral gift shop were very revealing. I realized that I saw my own journey as something special because I was traveling and exploring *alone*—I looked down on the packaged one-day tours led by guides reciting many facts and figures. But the experience was unique for each of us. We were all buying things that might somehow preserve memories of a significant occasion and become a way of sharing the experience with others important to us. I realized also that although I was enjoying my solitary travel, a companion would have enriched the adventure. The other shoppers seemed to share a kind of community. My irritation changed to a slight feeling of envy.

Thus mildly self-chastened, I went to sit quietly in the immense space of the cathedral's nave and to skim through my guidebook. As I read, it seemed difficult to separate St. Cuthbert from the building that was erected to shelter his mortal remains and memorialize his life. Cuthbert was born in 635, I learned, a time of extreme confusion two centuries after the Romans withdrew from Britain and left the settlers to fend for themselves. A former shepherd, he was renowned for his deep love and care as a pastor, confessor, and spiritual guide, and for his great learning in an age when ignorance was almost universal. Cuthbert is perhaps the most popular saint of the pre-conquest Anglo-Saxon church, endearing himself to his people by his willingness to dwell with them for weeks among the poor of remote villages. He would have preferred to be a hermit, but he was called as bishop and served thus for the two years prior to his death. He also would have preferred to maintain the ways of the Celtic church, but accepted the decisions of the synod of Whitby in 663 that the English church should follow the Roman practice instead.

Contemplating these historical details, I reached out my hand in the immense space to feel the coolness of one of the giant columns holding up the cathedral's superstructure. The building is not supported by the outside flying buttresses that typify Gothic architecture, but by the stocky internal columns I judged to be about eight feet in diameter. D. J. Hall's book on medieval pilgrimage has this to say about Cuthbert and his cathedral:

> The building represents the man remarkably: both in their separate ways are more than life-size, each has an austere simplicity, both disarm the doubter and critic with their warmth and holiness. The proportions here are perfect, the aesthetic balancing the ascetic, the

work of mind and body inspired. The immense pillars,
geometrically incised, give no sense of overpowering
weight.[1]

As I read on in the guidebook, I began to see the visitors
in the cathedral nave in a far different way from how I
had seen the tourists in the shop.

The building admits the world, and its great space
contains and orders it. Shuffle of footsteps, raised,
inquiring voices, the hard tap of heels on stone or
pattering boys, no crowded sounds can interrupt its
vast tranquility. It stands as did St. Cuthbert for divine
regulation in a world of chaos.[2]

The story of Cuthbert reminded me of my own longing
for order and predictability in my busy days. I thought of
the ways divine grace can touch my life—that despite
the violence and harshness in the world, God's grace
can work at a more fundamental level to restore
wholeness to creation, including myself.

After this I set out to enjoy Durham—its town center,
shops, hilly terrain, and especially the view of the
cathedral in its elevated location. The intent of the
city's leaders to accommodate many visitors is shown by
the streets that have been "pedestrianised," or so a
small welcoming brochure explained. Practically
speaking, it means that automobiles are excluded from
those streets near the small town square where foot
traffic is heaviest by upright sections of heavy steel
pipes placed in the pavement. This arrangement also
suggested to my more critical side that hordes of people

---

1. D. J. Hall, *English Medieval Pilgrimage* (London: Routledge &
Kegan Paul, 1965), 77.
2. *Ibid.*

regularly converge upon Durham and I should avoid the town square during peak tourist times!

In several directions from this central area, hilly terrain leads downward to the River Wear, whose meandering course almost doubles back on itself in the shape of a U. Over the ages the water has carved out a section of land like a peninsula, perhaps a mile long and one-third as wide, much of its perimeter a steep bluff that would have been easy to defend from a military assault. Sure enough, the shops and residences on top of this promontory are dominated by an imposing castle as well as the cathedral. It reminded me of those days when prince-bishops ruled over both secular and religious life, as a verse ascribed to Sir Walter Scott in my guidebook noted: "Grey towers of Durham. Yet well I love thy mixed and massive piles. Half church of God, half castle 'gainst the Scot."

Although a city, Durham has many of the marks of a small town. During my stay of only a day, I walked twice along a path bordering the river below the cathedral, once pausing to admire the skill of two teenaged boys paddling their kayaks through the water spilling over a weir. Visitors were few, and I felt that I could pause for long periods to enjoy details of the cathedral's structure without delaying others in their explorations. I was disappointed that the monastic buildings were closed to the public while being renovated, but found a warm reception from the staff of the Durham University library, located just beyond the cathedral's entrance drive. To my delight, the library was then featuring an exhibit that gave me new insights about the settling of America—this in the fifth centennial year of the journey of Columbus to the New World. The small town square was a pleasant place to sit in the sun among clusters of teenagers. The major attraction for youth seemed to be a rich variety of activities at St. Nicholas Church nearby, whereas people my own age inclined toward the quiet cathedral.

One day in Durham mixed time to myself and time for conversation with others; natural formations and the creations of human beings; activity and reflection. All these were part of a mixture of exploring the new and connecting it with what I had experienced in the preceding days and with preconceptions I had held before my travel even began. Only the week before I had spent three days on the island of Iona, thirty-five miles west of Scotland's mainland, after my day in Durham a whim drew me to Whitby, where a famous church synod took place in the seventh century. How did my choices fit together, and how did they lead to Durham? Perhaps my reasons are the same that have brought countless pilgrims in the past. A friend whose inclinations I trust spoke enthusiastically of the charm and historical importance of the city. My interest in Benedictine spirituality made me curious about the Celtic church, a tradition that is different from the Benedictine yet touches it in several ways. Another friend had told me, "The spirituality of northeastern England is different from that of other places; you will probably understand it only by visiting the area."

Visit I did. I remember reading the words of the cathedral dean that were posted inside the cathedral: "We warmly welcome our twentieth-century visitors and pilgrims to 'Cuthbert's Church.' Our prayer is that in coming to Durham Cathedral you will feel you have 'come home,' and that when you leave you will go on your way rejoicing." I was able to accept both invitations, still unclear whether I had come as visitor or pilgrim. Nor could I yet describe why I felt at home, but my sense of comfort there convinced me that I should like to visit Durham again someday.

☙❧

Questions for Reflection

What souvenir from a trip has been especially meaningful to you? Recall the circumstances of your acquiring it. Why did you buy or save it? If you still have it, what does it mean to you now?

When you are on an extended trip of your own choosing, do you prefer its format to be structured or unstructured? Why?

Generally, do you prefer popular or secluded places when you are traveling?

If you have visited popular cathedrals or attractions, how did it feel for you to be among a large number of other visitors there? What ways have you found to enrich your experience while in the company of others?

If you were setting out soon on a pilgrimage of your choice, would you prefer to be alone, with one other person, or in the company of a cohesive group? Why?

In what ways have your views of tours or pilgrimages been shaped by the experiences and comments of others? By books or articles?

Recollect a moment when you felt a sense of awe while sightseeing or on pilgrimage. Why did you feel that way? When have you felt that way before?

Chapter Two

The Pilgrim Impulse

Looking for God is like seeing a path in a field of snow;
if there is no path and you are looking for one, walk
across it and there is your path.

Thomas Merton

The two-week trip around Great Britain I have just
described led to three years of thinking about
pilgrimage: reading, recalling experiences not recorded
in my journal, imagining and speculating about
possibilities for future journeys. The extended period
has also proved to be an internal journey, one of
wide-ranging fancies, wonder, and study. In short, my
exploration continues in a very real way.

Much of the material I have found has focused on the
Middle Ages: diaries of travelers, descriptions of ancient
shrines, and records of how the medieval church both
encouraged and regulated pilgrimages. In the medieval
period pilgrimages became a way of life for two very
different reasons. Men and women longed to visit sacred
places, while the church also required arduous journeys
as proof that sacramental penances for sin had indeed
been fulfilled. One thing seems clear, however: medieval
history cannot be understood unless we comprehend
the importance of pilgrimage during that long period,

any more than our own culture can be understood apart from its great mobility and desire to explore.

I recently read an account of a contemporary journey retracing a popular pilgrim route of ancient times. The writer included short interviews with the pilgrims conducted along a lonely road, part of a five-hundred-mile trail in northern Spain. These modern-day pilgrims were walking to and from the cathedral at Santiago de Compostela, located in the northwestern bit of Spain that protrudes westward above northern Portugal to the Atlantic Ocean.

The hikers' serious intent was indicated by their garb. Most wore the scallop shells that have long been associated with the apostle James, who left his fishing nets in Galilee to walk with Jesus. The modern travelers' long wooden staffs, hiking shoes, layered clothing, and backpacks—especially the staffs and packs—placed them in the tradition of countless pilgrims who have walked the same roadways during a period of ten centuries. Their destination could be attained with hardiness and persistence, and they walked in relative safety, since the Moors were driven from Spain in the year 1031. Like the travel gear of their many predecessors, their provisions spoke of a commitment to reach an honored goal. And like pilgrims who had gone before, they would carry home some reminder or proof of their accomplishment—their shell badges, for example.

Not all European pilgrims of the Middle Ages looked toward the ornate shrine at Compostela. Literally thousands of other shrines were visited: far afield in the Holy Land, or in nearby places fifty miles or less from the homes of devout people who had neither the means nor the time to be away from their families and work for long. Only the hardiest and most reckless attempted solitary pilgrimages; the majority moved in groups that formed and reformed along the route. Some groups were, literally, armies. Eight crusades marched and sailed to the Holy Land over a span of nearly two hundred years, thousands of people bent on reclaiming the Holy Land for Christendom.

Most of the travelers seem to have been religiously motivated, either by choice or obediently working out penances imposed by church authorities. One of the earliest was a woman called Egeria who visited the Holy Land in the early fifth century; the record of her observations is still in print today. Egeria's residence for three years was Jerusalem, from which she journeyed to sites in Palestine, Egypt, and Syria. She sought to enliven her faith by seeing and walking around the holy places of scripture, particularly the sites where God spoke to the patriarchs and prophets, and meditating on the biblical stories. She was intent upon visiting sites mentioned in the first five books of the Bible: Abraham's home city of biblical Haran; Mount Nebo, the traditional place of Moses' death; the route that the Israelites took from the Red Sea to Mount Sinai. She traveled also to look at key places in the life of Jesus: places of his birth, ministry, crucifixion, and resurrection.

Egeria also visited several shrines that had been built by the emperor Constantine a century before her three-year pilgrimage began. Her heart was warmed by prayer with those faithfully living at and tending the holy places. One of her several accounts begins this way:

> I was told: "This is the city of King Melchisedech, and it used to be called Salem"...the place where Melchisedech offered pure sacrifices of bread and wine

to God, as it is written that he did in scripture. As soon as I heard this, we dismounted; and there was the saintly bishop of this place, and the clergy as well, graciously coming forth to meet us. After receiving us, they led us immediately up to the church, where, on our arrival, we recited a prayer right away in accord with our custom; then the proper passage from the book of the holy man Moses was read, and a Psalm fitting to the place was sung; and, after reciting a second prayer, we came down. When we had come down, the saintly priest spoke to us.[1]

In contrast, other medieval travelers sought a holiday or momentary respite from the strictures of hard life in an age when comforts were limited to a privileged few. Geoffrey Chaucer's fourteenth-century *Canterbury Tales* describes a typical group of pilgrims more given to pleasure than piety, and happy to forgo slow walking in favor of traveling horseback to the shrine of Archbishop Thomas Becket at Canterbury, in southeastern England. A mixture of the lighthearted and serious appears in an account called the *Evagatorium,* written by the Dominican prior Felix Fabri, who visited Jerusalem in 1480 and again in 1483. "The title itself," one historian tells us,

> was one of his pleasant but ponderous jokes. "I am resolved," he says in his dedication, "that this book shall not be called a Pilgrimage, nor a Journey nor a Voyage, nor anything else at all, but I have determined that it shall be truly entitled, named, and known as the *Evagatorium Fratris Felicis Fabri,* and we may translate that as we will by 'The Wandering' or

1. *Egeria: Diary of a Pilgrimage,* George E. Gingras, trans. (New York: Newman Press, 1970), 71.

'Rambling' or 'Straying of Brother Felix,' or perhaps by 'Friar Felix at Large.'"[2]

Truly eclectic, Friar Felix found the plants of the region as interesting as the ornate architecture. The well-preserved body of a saint moved him to astonishment, but his opinion of Jerusalem was less enthusiastic: "One beautiful building, that is its Mosque....I saw nothing else beautiful in the said city." Prescott adds: "Led about the usual tour of the Holy Places, he preserved his detachment....And it is quite clear that he enjoyed, far more than his trip with the friars, another day's outing when he was shown round Jerusalem by 'a very agreeable Moor.'"[3]

Devotion and the anticipation of pleasant diversion were evident incentives for venturing on pilgrimage. But the greatest single factor in the popularity of medieval pilgrimage was the search for healing. The powerful intervention of the saints was credited with a number of miraculous healings, and the reports of salutary outcomes increasingly attracted hopeful sufferers. In contrast to Chaucer's tradesmen and ecclesiastics on horseback, the poor and lame came with the help of friends or by their own labors. I can only begin to imagine the mixture of pleading voices, screams of the deranged, and joyous outbursts of thanksgiving when a band of pilgrims had attained their intended goal. The odors of unwashed bodies and ill-treated sores would surely jar the sensitivities of our age. Most likely the hoped-for peace and serenity beside

---

2. H. F. M. Prescott, *Friar Felix at Large: A Fifteenth-Century Pilgrimage to the Holy Land* (New Haven: Yale University Press, 1950), 2.

3. *Ibid.*, 31.

the shrine of a saint was soon dispelled by all the pushing and shoving to get closest to the bejeweled container in which lay some material relic of the departed holy one: perhaps a section of bone or skin, or swatch of cloth from a garment.

Those afflicted by illness or deformity streamed to the shrines with hopeful expectation in an age before medical arts were trusted or developed. Most people had heard of someone healed during or after the visit to a particular shrine; might the saint favor them as well? In time, church authorities began to take these claims seriously. We can still see in cathedrals and other revered sites the special observation seats from which monks could guard the relics from theft or damage, while also recording whether certain healings had truly taken place.

People are more likely to be impressed by physical wonders than by sermons or teachings. Furthermore, when they become wearied from hearing a vengeful God proclaimed from the pulpit, their natural reaction is to seek the mediation of the Virgin Mary or another of the saints believed to be more friendly and helpful. Through the hope of being healed, or simply preferring a direct and personal experience of faith rather than one mediated by the church, a period of eight or ten centuries was marked by devotion to departed saintly ones who could intercede for the supplicant to a transcendent and hidden God. In the Middle Ages, the search for heavenly intermediaries flourished. As the number of shrines increased, more and more people were honored by being proclaimed saints, true products of their age. Not surprisingly, there was even a brief period when a new church could not be consecrated unless it possessed some relic of the person in whose honor it was named.

The whole process of undertaking a pilgrimage was controlled by the rulers of both church and state. A pilgrim could not simply gather supplies and take to the road, whether the journey was voluntary or imposed as a penance by the church. Before leaving home, the pilgrim needed to obtain permission from someone in authority, clear up debts, mend unresolved relationships, draw up a will, make a confession of sins, and receive a blessing for the travel. True pilgrims were expected to wear or carry marks identifying them as pilgrims and not aimless wanderers or fugitive serfs, although these emblems were sometimes used as disguises by criminals preying on innocent travelers.

As medieval pilgrimage became more popular, church authorities imposed further regulations. Faithful members of the church could not begin a pilgrimage without church approval. In time, emphasis was placed on pilgrimage more as an act of penance than of devotion. Pilgrimages were used to discipline the wayward, and the bishop presiding over a shrine would have the power to authenticate the fact that the penance imposed back home had been cleared by the penitent's having reached his journey's goal. There were occasions also when one could pay a proxy to do the actual walking, much as mercenary soldiers could be hired to fulfill one's military service. Ironically, the intercession of deceased saints was replaced by living "pardoners," one of whom is described in Chaucer's "The Pardoner's Tale."

Detailed preparations were often the easiest parts of going on pilgrimage, however. Reaching the goal was quite another matter. A pilgrim site like Canterbury lay on the well-maintained route connecting London and Dover, and could be reached fairly safely and quickly. But less frequented or unmarked routes to other shrines could wash out in rainy seasons, forcing travelers to leave their paths and go into bogs or dense forest. If nature were not harsh enough, thieves could suddenly appear, or travelers might be coerced into paying for "protection" or advice. One safeguard for pilgrims was to visit the most popular shrines, near which they might depend on safety in numbers.

Word of mouth was the major source of helpful information, though guide booklets of recommended routes became available toward the end of the Middle Ages. The fifteenth-century *Informacion for Pylgrymes* was one of several books helping travelers on their way to Santiago de Compostela. It advised travelers on what to take on journey, foods to eat or avoid, useful words in a strange language, choosing a ship's cabin if a sea route was chosen, buying a bed, and fair prices to pay. Less prosperous travelers would be thankful for any adequate food and a safe resting place; often the traveler had to share a bed with other people, not to mention lice and rodents.

But helpful forces were also at work and responsive to this major movement in society. Monastic houses offered hospitality generously, and protective orders of chivalry such as the Knights Hospitaller and Knights Templar came into being to shelter vulnerable travelers. A pilgrim could expect the free gift of a day's food and bed at monastic hostels, and for a longer period if poor health overcame the traveler. In time, pilgrims could choose preferred routes and resting places, suggestive of the tourist amenities of our time.

As more and more people experienced firsthand the world beyond their cities or villages, other powerful forces began to grow in society. Pilgrims traveling together with hearts intent on seeing and touching the same holy shrine experienced a new level of equality, as people from a variety of stations in life banded together for added safety. Other travelers simply felt liberated from the routines of village life—perhaps to discover in some distant place, if only momentarily, what they imagined to be a moment of pure religious faith that was not captive to the church. It is likely that most travelers began to perceive the hugeness and diversity of the world around them in a way they had not imagined before, and were captivated by the allurements of markets and fairs clustered around the shrines. Arousal of the senses, new sources of interest and information, exposure to the arts, the promise of a new richness in life—all this would have powerfully affected people on pilgrimage no matter what their initial reasons for venturing from home.

A very significant element of pilgrim journey was that travelers came face to face with new realities. For the devout, the encounter might be a meeting with God, the transcendent Other. Pilgrims visiting a shrine might not only be healed, but undergo religious conversion. Pilgrimages came to be recognized as transforming journeys, and today we sometimes use the word to describe a journey which only in hindsight is seen as life-changing.

୬୯

What of pilgrimage today? The word itself describes a wide spectrum of experiences. Today's pilgrims travel to cathedrals, war memorials, cemeteries, and the places where their immigrant ancestors lived. They flock to athletic halls of fame, graves of entertainment idols, or places long hidden behind the Iron Curtain or the Berlin Wall. Devotees of Wordsworth travel to the Lake District in England, other pilgrims to Disney World in Florida, and still others to undeveloped countries whose way of life seems more enlightened than that of home. Individuals and groups converge on Lourdes in France, Holywell in Wales, or Graceland in Memphis, Tennessee. Nor are the pilgrim routes of today confined to Europe and America. All Muslim males are expected to visit Mecca at least once in their lives, while millions of Hindus visit the sacred places of India in a single year.

Tens of thousands gather spontaneously and reverently at the sites of tragedy, such as the 1995 bombing of a government building in Oklahoma City and the playing field in Enfield, England, where many fans died in the football arena's human stampede in 1989. Less spontaneous, but continuing over several generations, American family reunions are planned years ahead: same place, same weekend, year after year. Major religious sites remain honored after many centuries: Jerusalem and Canterbury, Rome and Guadalupe. Thousands of lesser known places are sites for pilgrimages in all regions of the earth.

Evidently several kinds of movement qualify as pilgrimage. A certain journey must be judged by the traveler to be somewhat different—and less ordinary—than other travel for some reason. Whereas our forebears joined medieval pilgrimages that were structured and approved by the church hierarchy, modern pilgrims are guided by individual temperament. Take, for example, St. Peter's in Rome or the National Cathedral in Washington, D.C. One person might walk there daily for a celebration of Holy Communion, while another on the same morning will have traveled several thousands of miles for a single visit. Still others, on a sightseeing tour of the vast cathedral, stop to gaze at the worshipers because they are aware that something alien to their own experience is going on and it makes them hesitate before proceeding.

If beauty is in the eye of a beholder, the difference between a pilgrim, a tourist, and a sightseer may also lie within the heart. Even today's weekend airline excursion to a newly developed Caribbean beach can be valued as a pilgrimage, just as were the medieval journeys through bandit-infested countrysides by large bands of people. Someone setting out to enjoy new sensations of sight or sound or touch may realize while on the journey that she has been transported beyond these immediate sensations to a level of deep feeling or religious aspiration. Another person may join a modern pilgrim band in order to seek release from an uncomfortable tie to the past, and either discovers a new freedom in the community spirit of the group or is so captivated by the scenic beauty en route that he abandons the original travel plan.

I recently searched my memory for the earliest experience I would now call pilgrimage. A journey I took with my parents when I was nine or ten years old came to mind, and several clear images quickly formed about the recollection. It was the memory of my parents' excitement as they planned to visit an old country church some twenty miles distant from our Kentucky home.

Some anxiety must have been mixed with their sense of anticipation. Though we four children were oblivious to anything but our own excitement, our parents might have viewed certain down-country hazards of travel in the same way oldtime pilgrims may have feared the prospect of bandits lurking off a popular route. What produced in my parents a sense of foreboding was adventure and excitement for us, which is a further reminder that distinctions among various kinds of journeys lie within the imagination of the traveler: tours, excursions, pilgrimages, larks, or mixtures of business and pleasure.

Our car was high-slung and able to ford two shallow creeks en route where bridges did not yet exist, but on one memorable journey it lost its battery, which jostled loose from an external mount on the car's running board and fell onto the surface of an ill-kept rock road. In that crisis, our seemingly calm and heroic father walked back, retrieved the battery, put it back in its place, and then resumed the journey.

After fording a wide-bed creek and scanning the roadway's weedy edge for several minutes, our parents spotted a narrow lane leading from the rock-bed road, and we triumphantly rolled up a lane into a grassy area alongside a group of horse-drawn buggies and automobiles partially framing a white-painted wooden church building. A growing band of children darted about, staying in constant motion. The potluck covered-dish dinner was eventually laid out on a few of the unpadded plank pews. We diners sat in front and back of the pews holding the food, reaching over now and again for replenishments. That memory is more vivid than the games we children played, but I do recall hoping that my father's eye and arm would prevail in an adult contest of pitching horseshoes, which clanked along an out-of-the-way side of the churchyard.

There was also a deeply emotional side to this occasion which I now recall but could not fathom at the time. Women and men joined in tidying the weedy graveyard near the church, and some of the adults stood looking down at the ground for prolonged periods while exchanging soft words. The small plot of the churchyard was a very important place of meeting, and the jokes and pleasantries of the day were dimmed for some of them by painful memories. Maybe that was really why they had come to the old country church and would continue to do so in future years: to reconnect with something that was sacred for them.

However, I gained quite a different view of pilgrimage a half-century later as my wife and I embarked on a program that brought us and thirty others to Canterbury Cathedral and several sites nearby in England. Making no claim to be either a tour or a pilgrimage, the sponsors of this program called the gathering an "experience." We participants converged on the cathedral by our separate routes on a designated date for ten days together. I had gone for several reasons, including a desire to become familiar with the titular center of the Anglican Church, reside within the walls that set the cathedral precincts apart from the city, and learn and live out some of the traditions of Benedictine life with others also committed to exploration.

Maybe I had anticipated the Canterbury visit as a pilgrimage because my understanding of that term includes a quest for something that has been venerable, holy, or sacred. I yearned not simply to visit a place, but also to live nearby and be able to enter and leave the cathedral as often as I wished, both day and night. I also wanted to take part in public worship and those times when our small group could be led silently in candlelight procession through the darkened undercroft so filled with shadows and tradition.

To my dismay, on the first two evenings Solemn Evensong was marred by the presence of a media crew recording the service for television. Those of us in the actual congregation were asked not to cough or scrape our feet on the floor of the spacious choir area where we sat, but to remain in place until the technical work had been completed. So what I had anticipated as the first authentic "pilgrimage" of my life began with what I might have expected on a movie lot—was I on pilgrimage in Canterbury or in Hollywood?

But this initiation was not without value and it helped me understand an interview I had read several years earlier of a young woman who visited the grave of her rock music idol every year. Her explanation for taking this annual pilgrimage was that in life he had been surrounded by other adoring fans and she could never get close to him, and assumed he was never aware that she even existed. At his graveside she could spend quiet hours on each of several days before returning to her distant home, aware that her deep feelings could be attended to further in future visits to the site.

Although definitions vary, there remains a strong common urge to be a pilgrim, as distinguished from a tourist or a sightseer. The view one holds of the journey is centrally important in shaping that urge. Evidently, some journeys focus on a goal while others are mere wanderings. I believe that an important mark of pilgrimage is its quest for something that is revered and sacred, whether it is Canterbury or the grave of a deceased movie star. The motivation for pilgrimage blends yearning with the conviction that attaining a physical objective will lead to a beneficial outcome for the one who has traveled expectantly to the particular site. At times there might be a strong hope or even confidence that through pilgrimage new energy will be unleashed in a life-changing way, or a problem that seemed unmanageable at home will be solved. This transition might become evident at the place of pilgrimage or grow slowly over ensuing months. Thus perseverance and receptivity to newness and change are part of pilgrimage, although initial wanderings may give way to a life-changing new directive, or what was viewed initially as a routine trip may become a pilgrimage. Often this is possible because an internal pilgrimage has preceded the physical one. One asks, "What is missing in my life? Could there be more? Would moving beyond my usual patterns change things for the better?"

In his *History of Religions* Victor Turner suggests that pilgrimages resemble rites of passage, similar to the formal recognition of coming of age or marriage. The passage is internal as well as external, moving from the ordinary and familiar to the new, leaving behind former constraints for the moment. One of Turner's favorite metaphors is that pilgrimage involves crossing a threshold and hence it is a "liminal" experience. Going to an unfamiliar location may provide new perspectives about the world, which in turn helps us to feel that we have entered something new that we shall continue to experience. Along with crossing into new territory, we enter a new realm in outlook. A common assumption is that if life seems not to be what it could be, a change of place will make it better. Generations ago, pilgrimage could have been distinguished from mere traveling or sightseeing by its focus on a desired outcome or goal, coupled with a format sanctioned by the church. The combination of goal and sanction gave a clear meaning to pilgrimage. A devotional pilgrimage not only fulfilled a life's longing or an imposed duty, but also set the returning traveler apart as a special person who had done a special thing demanding a substantial commitment. By contrast, the carefree wanderer was regarded with suspicion, lacking the social and cultural support that tourism and sightseeing now bestow. The more formal wandering of the Grand Tour of Europe was endorsed by Queen Victoria, however, as an important step in the enculturation of young men of the peerage. Ostensibly a preparation for a diplomatic career, it was also thought that if a young man was wild and inclined to run after women, he should do so abroad. Mere curiosity as the impulse for travel, however, was frowned upon by the church because it exposed the inquisitive and innocent to foreign lands and peoples. The church did not share the current idea that freely moving tourists in most areas of the world bring greater global understanding in both knowledge and human relations!

Today packaged tours and pilgrimage have largely reversed their roles, judging by the numbers of people involved. Commercial tours can be highly structured—oppressively so, some free spirits would suggest—and are certainly popular. Both forms of travel offer the opportunity to gain new perspectives about the world and self, even if they are undertaken with different outcomes in mind. But are there fundamental differences between pilgrimages and other kinds of travel that lead us far from home? Both can be initiated by a desire for change—of venue or way of life, of place or pace—from present knowns to possible not-yets. Either sort of journey may begin as a longing for rest and recreation; either can be planned in loving detail or begun on impulse; either can be taken alone or in groups which themselves may shift from casual to intimate.

There are important distinctions between pilgrimage and sightseeing that are primarily internal. Sightseeing seeks experiences that are different from the usual, such as change from the routine and familiar. Tourists move toward and beyond the borders of what they already know, expecting the new settings to be authentic—hence the respect for faithfully restored sites. Pilgrimage also leads one afield, but its search is for a new center in life, an internal change that is important enough to be sought from a remote setting, one we have heard of but not yet encountered. Sightseeing explores what is foreign, alien, and other, whereas pilgrimage seeks a new center for life.

ରେ

Questions for Reflection

In the fifteenth century Friar Felix was concerned about what to call his travels. What titles do you prefer for several important trips you have taken?

Recollect at least one journey that you might classify as pilgrimage. Has this view come in hindsight, perhaps from viewing the journey as including elements sacred to you? Did you set forth with a longing to reach a specific place, and with a belief that the journey would somehow satisfy at least part of your longing?

How would you distinguish among sightseers, tourists, and pilgrims? How would you describe some of the differences between sightseeing tours and pilgrimages?

Visualize a site that you hope to visit or revisit someday. What is its main attraction for you?

Why do you suppose that medieval church authorities sometimes prescribed pilgrimages as penances?

Why do you think the "tourist industry" has had such great economic growth in recent decades? Do you feel comfortable contributing to that growth, or do you seek out alternative ways of arranging travel?

ೞ

Chapter Three

An Island Pilgrimage

Carry us over the surface of the sea,
Carry us safely to a haven of peace,
Bless our boatmen and our boat,
Bless our anchors and our oars,
Each stay and halyard and traveler,
Our mainsails to our tall masts
Keep, O King of the elements, in their place
That we may return home in peace.

The Ocean Blessing

I have always been attracted to islands. Hence I am drawn to the voyages of Brendan, a popular Celtic saint and intrepid sailor who lived to be ninety-two and who, according to popular legend, reached the shores of America in the sixth century. Other accounts tell of his search for the "Isles of the Blessed," which led him and his companions among strange lands in search of the earthly paradise. There is a bit of Brendan's wanderlust in most pilgrims, I suspect.

The search for beauty, plenty, security, and a continuity with the past were by no means new to Brendan's time. Said to be an ideal as far back as the Bronze Age, the Isles of the Blessed were a goal for pilgrims for almost a thousand years. Some traveled by foot, or on horseback, some by ship, and some without ever leaving home. Island-dwelling Irish pilgrims could not walk from home to distant shrines, but felt called to yet-unfound places in the ocean's vastness. So convinced, some launched their fragile boats upon the water with the conviction that God would control the wind and waves and bring them to the islands for which they longed.

Nor were the hopeful sea travelers limited to those who were naive about ways of the seas. Some sought the New Jerusalem, others *Otro Mundo*—the other world. The journals of Christopher Columbus suggest that his first two voyages were marked by a deep trust in God's guidance, for he dated sightings of new lands according to the church calendar and named them after the saints and teachings of the church. The cluster of some forty islands and keys we know as the Virgin Islands, for example, were so named because their great number brought to his mind the tale of St. Ursula and the eleven thousand virgins who were martyred at Cologne while on a three-year journey prior to committing themselves to marriage.

I have felt an attraction to islands in every decade of my life. When I was nine years old I yearned to reach an island in the Ohio River across from where I worked on a family farm. Denied access for a couple of years, I immersed myself in reading about the imaginary islands in *Treasure Island* and the paradise prison of *Robinson Crusoe*. During my naval service in World War II, I discovered that peace is not merely the absence of war—and this I learned on a small islet within the harbor of Efate Island, in the New Hebrides of the southwest Pacific Ocean.

About fifteen years ago, I first visited the Caribbean island of St. Croix—Santa Cruz to Admiral Columbus and Holy Cross in English. I felt an immediate bond with the island: its trade winds, residents, vegetation, coral reefs, colors and smells, its mixed history, and much more. That began my continuing exploration not only of the island, but of the ways I was personally affected during twelve visits and the insights that came to me in my musing between times. I value small islands simply because they are places apart, as I value my own solitary times. Islands also have clear boundaries, another valuable reminder. Furthermore, islands are not free-floating—they are what they are only because they are connected to the rest of the planet, just as individual human beings can be who they are through their connection with the rest of humanity. My yearning to return to St. Croix is owing in part to the fact that each time I say farewell I leave part of myself behind, so that my return will be a joyful reunion with a place that has become dear to me.

The wandering two-week trip that took me to Durham and Whitby also brought me to another island—this time the island of Iona, the sixth-century home of St. Columba. Many islands lie off the western shore of Scotland, laid out like irregular pieces of a jigsaw puzzle waiting to be fitted together. Some of the islands are large, others tiny. The Outer Hebrides lie as far as sixty or seventy miles offshore, due west of the northern half of Scotland and well into the Atlantic Ocean. The Inner Hebrides hug the mainland, extending southward to within ten miles of Northern Ireland. Several of these inner islands have served as important stepping stones in culture's movement from Ireland to northern England and Scotland.

In the year 563, an Irish monk named Columba moved to the small Isle of Iona, some eighty miles distant from his native land. Smarting from accusations that he had plagiarized others' literary work, Columba led twelve of his brother monks to settle on the three or four square miles of Iona. The small island provided the necessities of life, light soil for raising crops on its west side, and grazing land in several areas. Good fishing was available for the men who had sailed from their homeland in circular hoop-and-hide coracles much like those used by a few intrepid sailors today. Iona's eastern side was well sheltered as a building site, and there the group erected a cluster of small circular dwellings similar to those built by tribal groups over the centuries. This clustering of small dwellings enabled a blend of solitary life and periodic coming together for worship and mutual aid in such matters as security and health.

In solitude, the monks could pursue their individual search for ever-deepening relationship with God. As a community, Columba's group saw its primary mission to evangelize the Picts, the resident culture from which the Scots evolved. From their base on Iona several of the monks moved out to establish other monasteries, and Columba himself traveled widely in Scotland and several times to Ireland. The island home setting allowed the deep rooting of a commitment which in time linked Irish and Pictish Christians: a commitment to impart the gospel message, to nurture study, and to express gifts of teaching and writing.

Seventy years after the foundation of monastic life on Iona, a call came from King Oswald for monks who could restore the Christian mission in northeastern England, where a pagan reaction had wiped out the fruits of earlier efforts. The monk Aidan led the new movement, starting in 636 on the still smaller island of Lindisfarne in the North Sea and then moving near the border of England and Scotland to spread out from there.

Repeated Viking raids forced the Iona monks back to the greater security of Ireland in the eighth century. But monasticism did not cease on the island. Several centuries later a new shape of monastic life began to emerge under the Rule of St. Benedict. From that point in time, a new band of monks lived together and shared worship several times daily. Their buildings were much larger than the old hermit cells, the new arrangement closely resembling the Benedictine configuration that was becoming common throughout western Europe. Thereafter the monks could sustain a balance of prayer, study, and work in close-knit community.

In an ironic turn of events, the existence of more accessible monastic houses in much of Britain meant that monks were seldom called afield as missionaries from remote Iona, as Aidan had been in the seventh century. But the abbey's influence continued to be felt locally and to attract visitors—sightseers, as well as pilgrims and artists in search of inspiration. By the early seventeenth century visiting antiquarians and preservationists reported that the island's ancient treasures were lying in ruins or disrepair, and preservation of the buildings began.

The aim of preservation of the buildings shifted to restoration early in the twentieth century under the leadership of George MacLeod, a Presbyterian minister from Scotland's mainland. Repairs begun in the late 1930s by a series of small summer work crews restored the thirteenth-century Benedictine structures to their former configuration. Today large groups of long-term visitors live, study, relax, and pray in these and larger facilities built somewhat later a walking distance away. Samuel Johnson's comment is still pertinent after more than two centuries: "That man is little to be envied...whose piety would not grow warmer among the ruins of Iona." Barren holy sites somehow aid our discovery of the need for devotional life as essential for true humanity.

ᎧᎧ

I came to Iona mindful of the variety of people who had visited and lived on the island: aboriginal Picts, Columba and his fellow monks, invading Vikings, Benedictine monks and Augustinian nuns, antiquarians, artists, tourists, pilgrims, and George MacLeod's group of craftsmen. My pondering the island's history was brief, for my senses soon took over. The first evening ashore I was caught up in the ethereal quality of the air washing Iona's three-mile eastern face. I found myself wondering whether the optical mystery results from low-angle sunbeams being lifted by sea water and returned downward by low clouds or fog, or whether there is another explanation. I already found myself wanting to share the island with others, though I had scarcely begun to explore it myself.

I was unaware at the time of my visit that William Wordsworth had also been fascinated by the curious light over Iona Sound, "extracting from clear skies and air serene, and out of sun-bright waves, a lucid veil." In the 1830s the poet wrote, "Iona's saints...garlands shall wear...while heaven's vast seas of voice chant their praise." But he did not enjoy being interrupted in his admiration of his discoveries: "How sad a welcome! To each voyager some ragged child holds up for sale a store of wave-worn pebbles, pleading on the shore where once came monk and nun with gentle stir." I can report that the latter distraction has apparently passed.

After taking several short walks to survey Iona's tiny village, the imposing abbey, and the rocky northern tip of the island, I joined a group of about sixty others on a guided hike around Iona. We passed through bogs, over rocks, climbed and slid over irregular terrain, and twice paused at impressive sites on the beach during our walk of seven miles. At the midpoint, I was relieved when our leader called a halt for lunch alongside a small hillock in the midst of a *machair,* or meadow, in the presence of grazing long-haired cattle. As we stopped I realized that many of the other walkers had not been carrying lunch, water, and an extra jacket as I had, and they cheered as a van appeared with their lunches on board!

What was the hike really about, beside acquainting us with the island? For one thing, I learned about how people and their animals live and work year-round in a sometimes harsh climate. On the humorous side, I crossed a nine-hole golf course that is apparently kept mowed by grazing sheep. Differing from familiar courses at home, here flags marking the greens lie flat on the turf rather than battle the vigorous wind. The course was laid out near the beach, and I instantly understood the historic origin of sand traps for a game originating in Scotland!

Several times I edged out of the hiking group to examine areas of turf that reminded me of Alaskan tundra in its springy feel underfoot. I walked aside to survey unmowed strips along fence rows, covered with flowers so small that I knelt down to observe them. Mosses and lichens covered rocks here and there, thriving in the moist climate. To my surprise, some of the areas also were abundantly dotted with tiny snail shells in four or five distinctive shapes. Time and again I turned to locate the sources of bird calls I had never heard before, or to choose the easiest way around rocky outcroppings in the gently rolling terrain.

During our walk I kept being reminded that the land on which our group walked is one of the very oldest exposed bits of Earth, a fact underlined by our descent to a beachside quarry that more than three centuries ago was supplying marble, mainly white with yellow-green serpentine marking. The altar in the abbey church is built of similar stone that was recently imported, in recognition of the fact that quarrying had been important in the early life of Iona.

The highest point of land on Iona is near the north end. Dun I's Cap, as it is called, rises just over three hundred feet above sea level, which I reached by a steep ascent at the end of the seven-mile hike alongside some energetic young people (without backpacks!). As it turned out, not everyone rose to the occasion, and the rest of us had adequate time at the hike's end to survey Iona and the landmarks over the water. I opened a map that included a circular inset with its center indicating the very point where I was standing. Around the interior of the circle were located outlines of the other islands you can see in silhouette from Iona. The Isle of Mull dominates the northeastern and southeastern quadrants, while the mainland town of Oban is about thirty-five miles away as a gull or gannet might fly, though too far away to be seen from the island. But the islands of Dutchman's Cap rested a bit west of north, and Staffa east of north, both clearly identifiable from their shapes in the compass directions noted on the map. Months later I would realize that personal, interior centering also becomes an important element in the experience of pilgrimage.

During my descent from Dun I's Cap, I had literally a bird's-eye view of buildings in the village and abbey compound. One section of the cloister's roof appeared to have patches of snow on the dark gray slate, and nearer at hand revealed many snow-white doves at rest. I have been told that Iona is their home, which is much in keeping with the coincidence that *columba* is the Latin word for dove. I should not have been surprised at this, for I had learned a further coincidence even before my visit. *Ioua insula* (meaning "island of yew tree") was confused in some ancient writings with the Hebrew Jonah (Iona), also meaning dove. It brought back to me the words of a psalm, "Oh, that I had wings like a dove!"

Back at Bishop's House where I was staying, I peeled off my hiking boots and checked more of Psalm 55. The words described my sense of release not only in my imagination, but in a deeply felt comfort:

> Oh, that I had wings like a dove!
>   I would fly away and be at rest.
> I would flee to a far-off place
>   and make my lodging in the wilderness.
> I would hasten to escape
>   from the stormy wind and tempest.
>   (Psalm 55:7-9, BCP)

During the next few days the words of this psalm brought home to me that even though I am not free from the busyness and complexity of modern life, a periodic movement into quietness is both restorative and exhilarating—and that I can choose to make such a release possible.

Iona's rhythms vary dramatically with the change of the seasons, accommodating a surge of summer visitors and then shrinking peacefully in autumn to about one hundred year-round residents, all of whom seem most hospitable. Short-term visitors, including many in their teens and twenties, arrive with the intention of living in church communities for a few weeks or for several months. Nor do day-trippers take the island for granted; indeed they impressed me as quieter than sightseers in other settings like Canterbury and Durham. I cannot explain their subdued behavior simply by the amount of time required to get there, even though it is considerable: by ferry from Oban on the mainland to the large Isle of Mull, then overland by coach, and finally by a second ferry one mile across Iona Sound. Three hours in each direction: six hours of travel for a few hours on Iona!

Perhaps it is Iona's ancient reminders of the past that help newcomers to shift so quickly into a quiet frame of mind. When first arriving at the ferry landing, you cross a three-block street with residences and shops on one side—this single road constituting much of the village. One block ahead on the right is the Augustinian nunnery, built at about the same time as the better known and much larger Benedictine abbey. Though classified as a ruin, enough of the nunnery remains to indicate the living quarters, the chapel, and the cloister flower gardens separating the two, and now tended by a local family committed to maintaining their beauty. Just beyond the nunnery and only one block from the village street, a right turn reveals the top of the abbey dominating the view two or three hundred yards toward the north. Nearer at hand on the left are the elementary school building, the parish church, and clergy residence—all simple and weathered buildings. The unadorned interior of the church reminded me of the several centuries of sternness in worship on Iona, and that clergy were not always available to minister to the island's residents.

My anticipation grew as I first approached the abbey, its blocky shape dark gray at that time of day, but sometimes appearing tan in other light. The interior is surfaced with similar rough-cut stone, though with pink colors adding to the warmth of a side chapel. On another evening I would sit cross-legged on the stone floor of the nave, worshiping with scores of others who had earlier claimed chairs for seating; but on this first visit I sat comfortably in a choir pew taking in a mixture of sights and my own wandering thoughts—among them my resolve to revisit Iona in company with my wife. I felt a strong desire to share the sense of well-being that arose not only from entering into the island's history but also from its particular geology—the fact that it is an island.

Seemingly undramatic events stand out for me on almost any journey—as if the ordinary is the base from which the extraordinary can arise. While on the group hike on Iona, I was deeply moved by a shared experience on the beach at small Columba's Bay. We were invited to choose and examine individual stones selected from the thousands on the beach. All sorts of hikers selected all sorts of stones: some pebbles, others substantial rocks. We were then asked to think during a few minutes of silence of something that had been troubling and to "give" our private worry to the stone we had chosen. Our guide then invited us to approach the surf and throw the stones into the sea, which signified the willing release of our burdens.

There followed many plunking sounds as each stone was thrown into the waves, but we were not yet finished with the ritual. Each of us was invited to choose another stone to leave as a token that our concerns had been released. We then silently and gently placed our stones on a mound, or cairn, that was already taking shape from past contributions as a sturdy memorial to the day. I can no longer visualize the stone I left, but I know that I left part of myself on the island in that simple expression of thanksgiving.

Iona broadened my view of pilgrimage, because the scenic and the sacred were thoroughly blended during my stay there. It reminded me that I can mix and choose between recreation, sightseeing, and pilgrimage. Each one is nourishing in its season. I also learned that pilgrimage need not follow a structured form, but can include simple wandering into new territory, as I had done on Iona.

Perhaps the loving work of restoration by George MacLeod and his fellow workers was itself a kind of pilgrimage, extending over twenty years, and journeying to and within a holy place. How solid and enduring is the finished restoration of the abbey's cloister and domestic buildings! Real people once lived there, and do again today. That realization warmed my heart.

MacLeod is said to have remarked that there are "thin places" on Earth whose ambiance reminds us that God is present alongside us as well as far beyond our comprehension. This idea of thinness suggests that overcoming our separation from God is easier in some physical locations than in others. I believe that God is as close to us in our homes and workplaces as over Iona

Sound, with the Ben of Mull casting its high background just a few miles away, but I can also be thankful for this moment of certainty about God's presence in creation, including this much prayed-upon island.

ᏦᎨ

Questions for Reflection

Visualize a place you have visited that represents an historical continuity that is significant to you. What does the place mean to you?

Do you feel a particular attraction toward mountains, seashores, lakes, forests, deserts, islands, or another type of natural formation? What basic characteristics of that sort of formation seem to underlie the attraction?

How do you think you would feel about living in a place dear to you that is seasonally visited by a great number of others?

Recalling the author's experience of casting a stone into Columba's Bay, try to recollect a simple ritual with others that gave lasting importance to your time together.

The author comments that "there are 'thin places' on Earth whose ambiance reminds us that God is present

alongside us as well as far beyond our comprehension."
Try to recover and describe such a sentiment in your
own life.

A pilgrim to Iona fifty years ago wrote a poem of blessing
about the island that begins:

> O ye angels of the Lord, bless ye the Lord,
>   praise Him and magnify Him for ever.
> O ye Saints of the Isles, bless ye the Lord.
> O ye Servants of Christ who here sang
>   God's praises and hence went forth
>   to preach, bless ye the Lord....
> O ye pilgrims who seek joy and health
>   in this beloved Isle, bless ye the Lord.

The pilgrim goes on to include the birds and animals of
the island, as well as the flowers and rocks and winds. If
you were to write a poem of blessing about a site you
have visited, for what aspects of the site would you
include?

Chapter Four

Warmth in Ancient Cloisters

Great care and concern are to be shown in receiving poor people and pilgrims, because in them more particularly Christ is received.

The Rule of St. Benedict

I have been considering a particular question for over thirty years: how to be *in* the world, but not *of* it, as the Christian scriptures exhort. It has engaged me in different ways, but the basic question remains: how do I savor life here and now without yielding the values and outlooks largely formed by the teachings of my religious tradition? I believe myself to be a unique creature of God, like every other human being, but I cannot stand apart from others. Living in society requires a variety of adjustments involving other people. Although I cannot live solely by other peoples' values and still remain unchanged, I must admit my need for the support of fellow strugglers. My desire for autonomy needs to be balanced by authentic relationship with others. I want to be myself, but not be excluded from community with others.

The question I wrestle with is by no means new. In his impassioned prayer recorded in the seventeenth chapter of John's gospel, Jesus comes close to the very words "in the world but not of it" (v. 16), as does St. Paul in writing to the churches at Rome and Corinth. The epistle of James counsels that pure religion involves keeping "oneself unstained by the world" (1:27). The support I need is, unavoidably, found largely "in the world," though at times I should like to place it squarely in God's lap. I sense that the most helpful course cannot be so simple as total dependence on others or on myself—or on God—but an interdependence.

The seventeenth-century poet George Herbert wrote that "living well is the best revenge." His words prompt me to ask, "Where have I encountered a time-tested example of living well?" One model I have long admired is that of Benedictine monastic life, which seeks a course between two extremes: neither denying God's bounty nor being consumed by earthly pleasures, avoiding both extremes of rigid asceticism and debilitating hedonism. Accordingly, I have read a great deal about St. Benedict and his Rule, participated in retreats, affiliated with a nearby abbey that I can visit regularly, and for years met monthly with a group similarly committed to the same monastery. For more than twenty-five years, I have lived according to a schedule that approximates the monks' daily routines: morning and evening prayers with my wife, regular reading of the spiritual classics, manual labor (working at house maintenance, in the grove of trees around our house, or in our vegetable garden), solitary quiet times at the beginning of most days, and striving to simplify my life while also engaging in professional work.

About ten years ago, I began to feel an attraction toward Benedictines beyond the local abbey, in other countries and other ages. I wanted to learn about how these monasteries spread beyond their Italian origin, to understand their impact on the culture of England and Wales, their inner workings, and their ongoing contribution to society. How could such a way continue for centuries and into the present day, when it seems on the surface to be so different from modern ways?

One of the first ancient monastic sites I visited was in northern Wales, where I was invited to join five others for an afternoon outing to the monastic ruins of Valle Crucis, a name I did not even recognize at the time. In a festive mood, we drove through the bustling town of Llangollen, then followed the River Dee's winding course for a while and were soon in the quiet countryside. I initially hoped that we would pause alongside the highway for a first and prolonged view of Valle Crucis Abbey, a large building that rises out of the rural countryside. The ruins of the abbey are situated in a meadow below the road, about two hundred yards distant, the shell of its large church structure at my near left and a fully enclosed building at the near right. I remained silent as our driver searched for a driveway into the site, appreciating the fact that he and the others were returning to a place they had already visited several times and wanted to share with us, while my wife and I were anticipating our first time there.

Built of gray stone, the L-shaped abbey ruins lie in a small valley beautifully proportioned to the shape of the buildings. Barren, sheep-dotted hillsides stretch away into the background, a striking contrast to the lush green acres of flat land around the building. A low wire fence now surrounds the ruined structures, some ground-level foundations in the near right-hand quadrant, and grassy areas in the rear where outbuildings once stood. The scene struck me as "picturesque" in that it resembled many pictures I had seen of other abbeys. Seeing the real thing validated what I had until that moment viewed only in photographs and drawings. I mentally touched antiquity, and a few minutes later added a physical touch as I moved my fingers over the rough-hewn stones and aging mortar at several spots on the walls. I tried to visualize people of the distant past who had lived there, and how I would have responded to the remoteness of the place and their austere way of life, had I been one of the monks.

My short reverie was broken as I looked just a few yards beyond the enclosure. Why did I become uneasy upon seeing a group of recreational vehicles parked near the rear of the fenced area, a score of tents staked in here and there, with vacationers and their dogs moving about? Did I think that for some reason my brief visit was more valid than whatever had brought the campers here for a week's holiday? While I was slowly examining the enclosure, they were outside at chores, games, and conversation. Selfishly I thought of how much I would have preferred the ancient site without its RVs, clotheslines, disposal bins, bicycles, frisbees flying through the air, and all the other reminders of modern recreation. Was I deluding myself, thinking myself to be a pilgrim simply because I had read extensively about monastic ways, whereas the others were "only vacationers" at an available and popular campsite? I decided to sort it out later. As it turned out, within the next year or two I came face to face with the historical evidence that ancient cathedral and monastery forecourts were primary places for these sorts of activities, and that abbeys often licensed merchants to rent space for annual fairs. For the moment, I decided to explore the physical site, still unaware that I was a beginner at understanding monastic life and buildings—and why people visit particular places.

The abbey of Valley Crucis is patterned after a number of others built during the twelfth and thirteenth centuries in Western Europe and Great Britain, in a basic layout that bound church and domestic buildings into a unit. About one-third of what I saw was the church on my left (northward) and two-thirds the domestic area to my right, or southward. A high pointed wall stands about fifty feet high close by the fenced entryway, punctuated near its top by a small circular window, at ground level by an arched door, and in the middle third by three large side-by-side arched window openings. This soaring wall is well preserved, a high monument in a green rural landscape, and the east wall at the far left stands as its counterpart some two hundred feet away. No overhead roofing remains, and only lush grass serves as a floor.

The church's north wall at the far left is today little more than a raised foundation, but the south wall extends much higher than I can reach. Within the now roofless church, I paused to imagine its residents gathering to worship God. Those known as choir monks gathered in assigned seats near the main altar to pray and sing praises to God on the average of every three or four hours each day. The lay brothers, often those working beyond the enclosure, gathered less frequently in the west end of the church, separately and as listeners to the words and music of the choir monks.

A gaping doorway at second-story level of one choir wall opens southward into the dormitory, down whose wooden stairway the choir monks would emerge in procession for 2 A.M. worship—part of an ancient practice traceable to Psalm 119: "Seven times a day I praise you" (v. 164). Trying to imagine how I would have reacted to such a discipline in the middle of each night, I began to notice how other features of the abbey's configuration might have accommodated the monks' lives in ways so different from my own.

Though the monk's life was dedicated to God, the entire day was not given to prayer and survival needs. The guiding Rule of St. Benedict calls for corporate and private prayer to be balanced with study and manual labor— and good works to benefit people living outside the cloister. Approximately four hours of the day were given each to prayer and study, and six to manual labor. The *horarium* was a timetable that specified the phasing of these three elements. The community was summoned for first prayers at 2 A.M., final prayers at about 9 P.M., and at five or six other times during a day. Rest and reading followed two of the prayer offices and work after three of them. Work typically was assigned for three periods, and meals were served in late morning and early evening—altogether a busy and rhythmic way of life.

The Valle Crucis structures are laid out to accommodate the several activities shaping each day. The church is well defined by its shape. The domestic building situated to the right of the church was where the community ate, slept, and carried out its life and ministry. The residence for the choir monks in the far right-hand corner is virtually intact, its two stories now covered with a sturdy slate roof—thanks to partial restoration in the eighteenth century when the location was occupied by a farm family. Visitors can climb a narrow, uneven stone stairway in this restored area to the large dormitory, then walk through its back wall into the abbot's apartment. Only foundation stones remain of a similar two-story wing for the lay brothers on the near right and for a single-story wing connecting the two dormitory wings—the intermediate area where food was prepared and eaten.

The three residential wings and the church's south wall enclosed the square green space of a small yard known as the garth. This open area was framed on all four sides by the cloister walkway, ten or twelve feet wide and formerly roofed but not walled on the garth sides. Silence was maintained in this central area where a number of the monks spent much of the day at study or performing the work of copying and illustrating manuscripts, sewing, repair work, and other chores. Monks who sat or stood to copy much-valued manuscripts could find some warmth and light from the southern sun reflected off the church wall. A small interior warming room was welcome at times—certainly on days when even the ink froze in the cloister area! Probably more active work beyond the cloister—in the fields or within the barn, mill, or brewery—was preferred when the weather was either very brisk or very pleasant.

The cloister walkway was valued also as a setting for meditation while walking. Here was a special place where monks seeking a closer relationship with God, enclosed as they were from the outside world, could meditate quietly during the course of each day. I paced several slow circuits around its gravel surface. While walking, it struck me that the monks' rhythmic life did not go in circles around the church, but instead traced an ellipse with two focal points: one their corporate prayer and praise in the church, and the other their individual work, meditation, and silent presence to each other in the cloister.

Thinking of this, I felt fortunate that I can enjoy my home in California but also find refreshment in far distant settings. True valuing of home as well as a place away from home means each can contribute to my treasuring of the other. So also can daily routines be enriched by obedience to the balanced way suggested by the Benedictine motto *ora et labora*, "prayer and work." For example, chapter 43 of the Rule of St. Benedict begins:

> At the hour of the Divine Office, as soon as the signal is heard, each one is to lay aside whatever he may be engaged on and hasten [to prayer] with all speed; yet with seriousness, so that no occasion be given for levity. Indeed, let nothing be preferred to the Work of God.[1]

Weary bodies could rest within the church in the period immediately following, while the petitions and intercessions offered at community prayer were carried back to the work places. So might anyone balance the two experiences of homemaking and travel, each most nourishing when valued alongside the other.

Circling the buildings, I came to a fishpond that served as an important source of food for a community that ate fish and fowl but not four-footed animals. The pond's far bank provided a fine vantage point from

---

1. *The Rule of St. Benedict*, trans. Luke Dysinger, as quoted in Norvene Vest, *Preferring Christ* (Trabuco Canyon, Calif.: Source Books, 1991), 116.

which I could admire the simple beauty of stone and vegetation, and take what became one of my favorite photographs featuring the high pointed east wall of Valle Crucis Abbey.

Still farther from the church is the creek, which played an important part in the health and industry of the monks. As was true of many old monasteries, a continuous supply of running water was diverted upstream from the creek into a stone-laid conduit passing through the fields to the cloister area, thence alongside the kitchen, below the latrine, and into the creek at a lower point. The creek also provided water power for a mill used initially for grinding grain, and later, in the heyday of sheep-raising, also served as a pounding mill to wash and thicken the wool. It reaffirmed my initial impression that the abbey was both self-contained and different from the loose grouping of buildings common in earlier monastic communities. The reason lay in an orderliness that the Norman invasion brought to the island in the late eleventh century. One visible contribution to monastic regularity was a standardized layout for the buildings: a church of major proportions bonded to the domestic buildings by way of the cloister.

By the year 1201, when the abbey's construction began, a basic architectural pattern had been well established for monasteries of the Benedictine and Cistercian orders. (The Cistercian order was a reform movement with stricter observance of monastic practices.) Materials and money came from both ecclesiastical and secular sources for construction of Valle Crucis. In the way monastic houses were typically founded, monks from Whitland Abbey in southwest Wales built Strata Marcella, a daughter house some ninety or so miles away, near modern Welshpool. Valle Crucis Abbey, about twenty miles still farther north, came next in line, granddaughter of the Whitland community. Financial support came from the Welsh princes attracted by the monks' ability to convert barren areas into fruitful land. Significantly, the abbey takes its name from "the valley of the cross," a ninth-century pillar standing nearby in memory of the last ruler of the principality of Powys.

Out of often barren or boggy sites needing first to be drained, new health and culture emerged in hundreds of monasteries that attracted people seeking the religious life. In time, villages formed close at hand to monastic communities throughout Great Britain. Communities of men and women observed the disciplined and rhythmical life of prayer, work, study, and hospitality, keeping these ideals alive for many centuries. Earlier the Roman Empire had collapsed after being sacked repeatedly by barbarian invasions from the north, its former cities scenes of violence as society suffered massive collapse in the form of poverty, illiteracy, homelessness, and unemployment. Monastic women and men did much over the centuries to recivilize society by establishing hospitals, orphanages, libraries, schools, apprenticeship for crafts, and a life of order within the cloister. This period in history provides a dramatic example of how a rediscovery of balance between active accomplishment and intentional quiet reflection can raise up a new quality of life today.

୬୯

Understandably, these centers of renewal attracted around them many people who chose not to live as monks, and they constantly risked being absorbed into the secular culture. The Cistercian movement, which began at the end of the eleventh century, turned from the increasingly active ways of its Benedictine parent of sixth-century origins by returning to an emphasis on intercessory prayer, silence, and an increased simplicity in vestments and diet. Most visibly, the Cistercians chose to live in remote locations that would support these reforms. However, this lifestyle proved to attract even greater numbers of monks, and called for the construction of large facilities.

Valle Crucis was a small abbey in Wales. Several very large and striking Cistercian monasteries were located in Yorkshire, in northeastern England, and I resolved to visit Rievaulx Abbey there. My first trip to Rievaulx was by bus in the company of two dozen fellow travelers whom my wife Norvene and I were conducting on a two-week exploration of monastic sites. Our bus was wide, the roadway narrow and steep. For the last couple of miles we rode slowly past trees and bushes overhanging the road, a few houses, and an old church building—and there it was, an immense stone shell looming out of the morning mist in a small valley. Like the buildings at Valle Crucis, these seemed snugly fitted into a valley alongside the River Rye, though here much greater in number and size. My enduring impression is the remoteness of the place, which seemed to be a requisite for Cistercian monastic life.

After three additional visits in later years, I am still much impressed by the size of Rievaulx Abbey. One first impression I had is still revealing. When my wife asked me what I was thinking, I responded, "It reminds me of an aircraft carrier!" The place seemed self-contained at one end of an expanse of land, and the very long, roofless church was long enough to suggest a flight deck.

There are countless nooks and crannies both in large abbeys and large ships, and I set out to locate the treasury, library, infirmary complete with its own chapel and cloister, reception parlor, fuel storage, water system, and the warming room—the only place set aside for restoring comfort to those working in the cloister or elsewhere in frigid weather. The graceful immensity of the structures, with a length of nearly four hundred feet and height of perhaps seven stories, caused me first to stand motionless in awe. The obvious great age of the structures seemed to abolish all time frames, and I wondered whether I would discover some new appreciation for the ongoing movement of years in my life. Before leaving the ruins, I lingered to enjoy the sunlight on the half-acre of cloister lawn. I realized too that imagining myself back into the twelfth century had lessened my concern about what our group would do next, and I saw that my pilgrimage had drifted from sightseeing to a sense of timelessness, and that these memories would let me cherish Rievaulx Abbey long after my travel there had ended.

Rievaulx was active about seventy years before the founding of Valle Crucis. Under Abbot Aelred it was home to one hundred and forty choir monks, in contrast to about thirteen at Valle Crucis, and at least five hundred lay brothers, so it "swarmed with them like a hive of bees," according to Aelred. I asked myself, what forces could have brought so many together to live in community?

One answer would be personal response to divine call, especially in an age when the vowed life was perceived as much holier than the secular, and earthly life primarily a journey to the heavenly. Doubtless, others sought dependable care for the body as well as the soul, food and protection for both. Monastic life promised a release from the violence of society, and movement from chaos to order. It also offered a life of relative independence for women, as well as an education. Women's communities would certainly attract women—both widows and the unmarried—who wanted to escape being the property of their male relatives or who feared the perils of childbirth in that age.

Yet another consideration: numbers beget numbers, and so the presence of family members within monastic ranks encouraged their relatives to don monastic habits as well. Not only the young became nuns or monks, but a range of ages: a nurse to a baron's children now grown, knights claiming their allegiance to the cross rather than the sword, survivors orphaned by plagues and seeking a new sort of family. I suspect that it would seem natural for monks and lay brothers or sisters living within a magnificent structure to feel that they were connected with something important—bigger than life, yet yielding a new quality for life lived simply.

The Middle Ages were evidently the great years of monastic culture, which can be appreciated today in thoughtful exploration of both simple and elaborate sites. But it would be a mistake to conclude that the cloistered way was totally independent of life "outside." Often the wealth of great landed families funded construction of the largest monasteries, and such families sometimes gave holdings to the monks rather than let them fall into the hands of their rivals. Furthermore, the same systems of commerce and exchange affected all of the population. The breakdown of the agrarian-based feudal system was nearly complete by the end of the thirteenth century, and workers formerly hired by monasteries moved into the newly forming cities. Devastating plagues commencing in the mid-fourteenth century affected people in all walks of life. Thus several powerful forces rapidly reduced monastic populations. Then as now, monasteries and parish churches were part of the same economic and political systems as every other institution. They were in the world and part of it, both threatened and influenced by the values of the world "outside."

On several group visits to both Valle Crucis and Rievaulx, I began to ask the question, What brings people together for a pilgrimage? I became aware of a shared eagerness to venture forth in a structured way with people whom they trusted as leaders—someone to walk with, and no overwhelming surprises! They valued the assurance of a balanced experience: time for quiet reflection as well as activity, and freedom from pressure to be constantly on the move from one location to another. At least half of my companions expressed their hope of deepening an inquiry they were already making into Benedictine life. Always there are those seeking to be part of a caring community, even if it is of short duration. Mainly, their desire seems to be for something not evidently available at home, and the opportunity to search in the company of others who value and affirm similar interests. The search often begins simply: someone steps away from "life as usual" in order to consider other time-tested possibilities.

After my first visit to Valle Crucis, I was moved to reappraise my own life. How might I adopt some of the helpful practices in my own century from which my daydreaming could not really rescue me? The communal aspect of Benedictine life helped me recognize that such contact is important because it vitalizes me, and so I have increasingly valued my worship with fellow members of a parish congregation and participation in two small support groups beyond the parish. My struggle to live simply was also validated by my exposure at Rievaulx and Valle Crucis to the simplicity of those who lived seven or eight hundred years earlier than I. My hobby of vegetable gardening became even dearer to me. Noting the small niches that had accommodated entire monastic libraries, I realized how much I treasure the multitude of books readily available for my use. I could admire ancient architecture even if living in it would have uncomfortable for me. So an ancient, tightly-knit, now invisible, community touched my life in a surprising number of ways. My resolve deepened to appropriate as many lessons from monastic life as I could fit into my here and now. Altogether, I realized that I cannot escape my century, but that I can be aware of God in the present and in details of everyday life.

Facts and analysis fascinate me, especially when I am beginning to explore a new interest. Books serve that purpose for a while, but if the interest continues I want to be there—to explore it myself, in person. Enduring, long-term impressions come gracefully, without any effort on my part. At Rievaulx Abbey on our first visit, Norvene and I walked toward the entry gate to inform the members of our group about the ongoing schedule. A young cat was sunning herself nearby; rangy and adolescent, she still had the playfulness of a kitten and invited us to join her. Three years later, on our return to Rievaulx, the same cat sauntered up to us. This time she did not ask us to play, but at least expressed a formal willingness to be approached—as long as we did so with proper reserve. A warm bond was added to my interest in stones and history that make a place interesting.

Since then we have been able to visit Valle Crucis on several occasions. One sunny day we drove there with two of our closest friends. It seemed right that we four should offer thanks and celebrate how special to us is our commitment as oblates of St. Andrew's Abbey near our California homes, and how we honor those who for centuries have kept alive the monastic tradition. We celebrated Holy Communion on the ancient footing of one of the four side altars that frame the remnants of the central high altar, juggling a plastic cup of wine and a traditional English biscuit on a linen handkerchief upon the irregular surface of stone and mortar. The seats were uncomfortable, but the noonday sun was bright and the fellowship still warmer.

As I began to refold the handkerchief serving as our altar cloth, I became aware that the moss covering parts of the stone foundation was in bloom. Yes, moss blooms—in this area with tiny stems more than an inch long and only slightly thicker than fine threads. The tiny clusters of spores resembling flowers were reaching toward the same sun that was warming us. I have heard that patches of lichen, a relative of moss, have endured in harsh climates for more than two thousand years. Perhaps this same moss has clung to a firm foundation and lifted its blooming praise for centuries—and might even be there to greet us if we ever return.

❦

Questions for Reflection

Imagine yourself living in a former era that has held your fancy over the years. What elements about that age attract you? How do you incorporate them into your own life?

How would you describe your views of monasticism to a close friend?

Sometimes our images of a place come first from pictures, rather than a visit in person. Are there places you have visited only after first being attracted by pictures of the site? How did the actual place differ from what you had envisioned? How was it the same?

What adjectives best describe your view of true community? When and where have you experienced that kind of community?

The author describes feeling taken aback at first seeing many campers alongside Valle Crucis Abbey. How have you felt to discover crowds of visitors at one of your favored places? How did you find a way to share in the experience of the place with them (or despite them)?

ଓଔ

Chapter Five

Pilgrimage Through a Library

You never enjoy the World aright, till you see all things
in it so perfectly yours, that you cannot desire them any
other way: and till you are convinced that all things
serve you best in their proper places.

Thomas Traherne

A taxi trip from the Chester railway station convinced
me that when one is driving on the left-hand side of
the road, left-hand turns can be made as smoothly as
right turns in my own country. We had scarcely driven
the seven miles to the Welsh village of Hawarden when a
turn into Church Lane revealed St. Deiniol's Parish
Church beyond a cul-de-sac a hundred yards ahead.
Another left turn from that point put us in front of St.
Deiniol's Residential Library, which has no official
connection with the church although both are named
for the same sixth-century Celtic abbot-bishop.

My immediate thoughts were not on historical facts,
however. Memories from my past reading called up
images of the stately buildings featured in the Victorian
novels of George MacDonald, who was so valued by
other authors of fantasy like J. R. R. Tolkien and C. S.

Lewis. Those images became move vivid as Norvene and I were formally but warmly welcomed beyond the massive oak front door. We were courteously escorted to our room: up a grand oaken staircase from the ground floor to the first floor, then along a hallway across half the width of the large H-shaped building, a turn into a smaller stairway and up another flight of stairs. Then two more turns into other short hallways, and down a single step into a garret room—a fine spot set apart for would-be authors!

We had reached the world's only sizable residential library, a memorial to the Great Britain's nineteenth-century prime minister William E. Gladstone. En route to our room we encountered a half-dozen reminders of him in the hallways and stairwells, and on a spacious windowsill: pictures, statues, cartoons, and chinaware. We would daily see other items reminiscent of the prime minister in the dining room, common room, and library reading room, and hear him respectfully and consistently referred to as Mister Gladstone.

Dinner was being served when we reached the library, and we were soon seated in the large dining room next to our host, who spoke with an undiluted Yorkshire accent conveying mirth and abundant energy. I felt heartily welcomed from the very start of our proposed four-month stay, and for the moment was able to thrust aside the dull residue of jet lag after our journey from America.

Immediately after the meal, we diners reconvened for coffee and tea in the common room a few steps down a hallway. That airy room proved later to be a cultural crossroad and center for daily sharing of ideas and fellowship. Within the next few days we would learn that some dozen staff and thirty visitors from Great Britain and beyond were there as well, having an array of plans and expectations: to read deeply in a single subject, to write an essay or book, perhaps to study for examinations for degrees in the nationwide Open University, which includes students over a wide age range. All seemed attracted by the peace and quiet of the place, or worked there to help create its restful environment.

St. Deiniol's is not a public library, but a large residential research library with room for forty-six people. A formal introduction is required: residents cannot simply drop by and stay, but must be commended in writing by someone in public office or by an established "reader." There the formality ends. To my mixed surprise and delight, I could extract a book from the high array of shelves and take it to our room, simply recording brief details on a pad of paper and depositing the sheet in the empty space left by the book. With similar freedom, I could leave a stack of books selected for my continuing use on a library desk, unconcerned about their removal. These details I learned by the end of the second day. Meanwhile, my dominant sensation was the distinctly bookish smell created by paper, ink, and leather bindings, all well blended and aged to proclaim, "Books, and many of them, old and new!"

The spacious gallery of the high open room became a place where I could immerse myself in a writing project at least five mornings of the week. From my desk on a balcony overlooking much fine carved oak wood, I could browse along the shelves for shorter afternoon and evening periods when my energy and the inclination to write had waned. Indeed, browsing became a major mode of exploration, for the library's filing system was different from any I had encountered elsewhere. Books are still shelved in the same categories Gladstone used for the thirty thousand volumes he moved to St. Deiniol's from his nearby home study, which he called his "Temple of Peace." In fact, a number of the older volumes clearly show marginal notes and comments he wrote more than a century ago.

This filing system, initially puzzling and inefficient when I was eager to get on with my work, led me into subject areas I might not otherwise have explored. Ambling through the books revealed all sorts of fascinating facts and curious commentary. Perhaps more important, the retrieval system was effective in curbing my urge to move quickly into the writing task I envisioned, while it also added helpful nuances to the topic I was exploring—the spiritual roots of stress. I was led to recall a comment I had read years earlier by Ralph Waldo Emerson, that good readers make good books. Slowing down was perfectly acceptable—and pertinent to my chosen topic!

My love affair with books is a long one that emerged during junior high school days. For two years of our adolescence, my brother and I reported each school day not to a classroom but to the library as our "home room" where we heard assorted announcements and settled down before classes started. As an assistant to the librarian, I felt that I had "first dibs" on books, and could leaf through a variety of titles and select those arousing my curiosity or promising to entertain. Years later I saw the truth of the maxim that knowledge is power and that it can come directly through information—presumably information that others had not yet learned. Meanwhile I was under the influence of books as guided by our friendly librarian, Miss Sloan. Jean LeClerq, scholar of the monastic culture of the Middle Ages, gives quite a different motive for reading, however. In his book entitled *The Love of Learning and the Desire for God*, he holds that the monastic literature of the Middle Ages aimed to increase and to communicate the desire for God:

> Well into the middle of the twelfth century, in the midst of the flowering of scholastic theology, while minds were incurring the risk of getting lost in side issues, the abbeys remained conservatories, as it were, of the great Christian ideas.[1]

Monastic communities from as early as the second century considered books to be essential for the spiritual life. Monastic schools grew up in Christian Ireland, and in their *scriptoria* both pagan stories and legends of the saints were preserved. According to the Venerable Bede, many "pilgrim scholars" were drawn to these schools from Britain and Europe. Bede wrote:

> In the course of time some of these devoted themselves faithfully to the monastic life, while others preferred to travel round to the cells of various teachers and apply themselves to study. The Irish welcomed them all gladly, gave them their daily food, and also provided them with books to read and with instruction, without asking for payment.[2]

---

1. Jean LeClerq, *The Love of Learning and the Desire for God: A Study of Monastic Culture* (New York: Fordham University Press, 1985), 106.

2. Quoted in Edward C. Sellnmer, *Wisdom of the Celtic Saints* (Notre Dame: Ave Maria Press, 1993), 22.

The Benedictines recognized the importance not only of reading, studying, and explaining the works of "the church fathers," as the earliest theologians of the Christian church were called, but also of trying to model their lives on the wisdom these treasured writings contained. Most monasteries had their *scriptoria,* where monastic and lay scribes and artists copied and illuminated the manuscripts. Among the more famous of these were St. Benedict's sixth-century monastery in Monte Cassino and Bede's own seventh-century community in Jarrow. This commitment to preserve and extend access to books continued with the Cistercians onward from the eleventh century. Jean LeClerq writes that St. Gilbert, "in an observation which has since become famous, said that St. Bernard and the Cistercians had 'renounced everything save the art of writing well.'"[3] The Rule of St. Benedict refers to its library, specifies that individual reading is expected of each monk during Lent, and requires intensive daily study periods for the monks lasting about four hours per day.

As demanding as this regimen may sound today, production of a single book during most of the Middle Ages required equal commitment of time and care under less than optimum conditions, including bad weather and dim light. (Recall the exposed cloister work areas at Valle Crucis and Rievaulx.) Nor was the project inexpensive despite an abundance of "free" labor; parchment for a single copy of the Bible required all the hides from a large flock of sheep! Understandably, the offering of a completed book was done in the spirit of a thanksgiving liturgy, and careless

3. LeClerq, *Love of Learning,* 113.

treatment of a manuscript could result in strict disciplinary action.

But back to the present century. There I was, actually living in a building that housed about two hundred thousand books and pamphlets, plus a bindery for the restoration of precious texts! How could I appropriate this treasure without falling victim to my natural inclination to sample a bit of everything? Three factors came to my rescue. First, I was officially on a sabbatical study leave and striving to conform to a preconceived plan. A last-minute change also had to be factored in, for my four-month sabbatical was suddenly shortened to two by the death of a friend who was also my senior colleague. How could I get near to my project goal without pushing to the point of fatigue?

A second source of help was the structured routine of the residential library itself, to which I immediately adapted: rising, morning chapel service, walking about the village or planning the day's work, breakfast, intensive writing, morning coffee in the common room, more writing, lunch, and so on into the afternoon. The resulting discipline was liberating rather than constricting. I related the comfortable schedule to the way a monastic *horarium* divides the monks' day into repeatable segments that overall provide a helpful rhythm.

A third support for my writing effort came from beyond the help provided by others or the prior expectations which had brought me to St. Deiniol's Library in the first place. As first unconsciously, but later intentionally, I began to view my time as a *sabbath* rather than mere "sabbatical" study leave. Increasingly I thought about what was special—yes, even sacred—about time. I had been attracted for years to sacred places and to stories about the lives of holy people. But the passage of time during my own life span, whose duration was unknown, had also to be consecrated. I began to see the importance of Abraham Heschel's comments in our century about the meaning of sabbath. Heschel wrote that primarily sabbath is to celebrate time, to share what is eternal, and "to turn from the results of creation to the mystery of creation; from the world of creation to the creation of the world."[4]

Happily, as it turned out, I did accomplish what I had hoped: I moved beyond the initial outline to the rough draft of a full book. Granted, many refinements would be necessary, but a sense of passing over an unseen threshold came to me, somewhat as on winter-weary days in my childhood I suddenly knew with certainty that spring was on the way. In a similar way I realized that I was getting somewhere important and that further persistence would most likely yield an acceptable product. In *The Writing Life,* Annie Dillard captures that moment this way: "From the corner of your eye you see motion. Something is moving through the air and headed your way."[5] The excitement began to build steadily from that sharp moment in the library—just as, I suspect, pilgrims over the centuries have been renewed upon detecting signs of their final destination that are different from markers seen earlier on the journey. These pilgrims' commitment to the journey more than likely deepened their awareness of each new signpost along the way.

---

4. Abraham Heschel, *The Sabbath* (New York: Farrar, Straus & Giroux, 1981), 10.

5. Annie Dillard, *The Writing Life* (New York: Harper & Row, 1989), 75.

Among St. Deiniol's extensive collection of books, I came truly to believe that I could be faithful to my desire to write while observing sabbath even if the completion of my task should be delayed. Thus relieved, I began to see my time in a different way; I saw that I was on a pilgrimage to honor myself as well as my work. Among thousands of books with their vast stores of information, I became receptive to my ongoing spiritual formation as well as to my gathering, consolidating, and (I hoped) imparting information.

I doubt that I should have found the library so attractive if it had been located in a noisy urban setting. But verdant countryside is all around Hawarden, and public footpaths crisscross the area every few hundred yards. I walked most of the cross-country ways, some a dozen or more times in search of the blackberries growing in hedgerows to share at breakfast. Not simply walking for exercise, I was also exploring the village. The remains of an old grain mill lie alongside a creek in a wooded area downhill from ancient Hawarden Castle, which formerly overlooked the main transport route from Chester to North Wales. Rock walls define the major estate, and small shops line several spots along the narrow highway that is crowded with traffic during commuting hours. I believe that at one time a single road sign at the center of the village pointed out three alternate routes to nearby Chester!

That well-signed crossroad is a small traffic roundabout with an inactive fountain at the center, predictably dedicated to William E. and Catherine Gladstone. Row houses along the narrow highway north of the fountain date from the 1870s, and an assortment of businesses and homes continue southward near Hawarden's single traffic signal at a pedestrian crosswalk. Three pubs are located in the stretch of a single block; one, the Fox and Grapes, is affectionately referred to as a place for "choir practice" after a quiet day poring over books. Altogether, my daily walking explorations were a helpful relief from intense work of reading and writing.

Browsing the village was as important as browsing the books, and both were a journeying within myself. I felt as accepted by villagers as by the librarians. One veteran of World War II, simply from overhearing my accent, told me how helpful American aid had been during those hard years. A gardener who let me work among his flowers took us to an ancient church, where a very old tower clock is still activated by the weight of a carefully chained boulder rather than a cast iron piece. One group invited me to test my aptitude at bowling on the green, and families invited us for afternoon tea. During a particularly cool week in our late summer visit, we asked a shopkeeper when summer comes to North Wales. "July," he said emphatically, "every other year!" In later visits, some of the residents came to recognize us from year to year and say, "Back again, I see. How have you been?" Generally speaking, both the comment and the question are good for introspection when on pilgrimage of any sort: "How has life been for me up to now, and how would I like it to be in the future?"

At the end of our two-month sojourn, we spent our final day in southern England so that we could take a morning flight home to America. While breakfasting in a small London hotel, we shared our delight about actually having begun to write in a committed way. On the other hand, we wondered whether we had missed important experiences by not having traveled more widely while in the alluring Welsh countryside. Our question was partly answered by the others who were there for breakfast: four people at one table talking to a pair seated halfway across the room. It was also their day of departure, and the major topic was fatigue. Their two itineraries were different but the outcome similar: much travel and a bewildering fuzziness about what they had encountered, and where, and when. Later my wife summed it up for us both: "We didn't visit all of Europe, but Great Britain came to us at the library!" The gift of experiencing warm community for two months had won out over our wanderlust.

Our hour in the London breakfast room proved memorable, quite apart from the tasty kippered herrings that compensated for the well-cooled toast. Since that morning when the reality of departure finally hit, we planned to return to St. Deiniol's Library and the village of Hawarden. Moreover, we wanted to share that setting with others: to use it as our "home base" from which to visit other sites. Two or three years thereafter seemed like good timing, and Benedictine heritage a good theme. We would need to do more study and substantial planning before we invited fellow pilgrims, but we left the hotel for Heathrow Airport resolved to return to Wales and the people and places that had received us so graciously.

Questions for Reflection

Many people like to browse: at yard sales, fabric stores, libraries, on the Internet. What are your favorite ways to browse? What makes them enjoyable to you?

Sabbath could be described as the time when one ceases the act of creating in order to marvel at the creation of the world. What have you discovered to be your best way of observing regular sabbath?

Recall when you were working at a puzzle or other challenge, and sensed suddenly that you had "broken through" the tangle. What did it feel like? How did it change your approach to the challenge?

What has been most refreshing about substantial journeys you have taken, and what most wearying?

Driving on the left-hand side of the road seems at first counterintuitive to Americans visiting other countries. What customs or traditions elsewhere have caused you initial concern? How did you adapt to them over time? How did you feel about them by the time you left?

Chapter Six

A Pilgrimage for Healing

In a country without saints or shrines
I knew one who made his pilgrimage
to springs, where in his life's dry years
his mind held on. Everlasting,
people called them, and gave them names.
The water broke into sounds and shinings
at the vein mouth, bearing the taste
of the place, the deep rock, sweetness
out of the dark.

Wendell Berry

A common motivation for setting out on pilgrimage can be summarized by the simple declaration, "I want to go. I feel that there might be something there for me."

Medieval pilgrimages sprang from a variety of motives, as we have already seen, but acting out of these several impulses always brought at least one common outcome: exposure to otherness. Pilgrims throughout the ages have encountered different and far away places, objects, people, and customs, finding them to be more vivid than they could ever have expected from the descriptions and reports of others—often far beyond what they could even have imagined. New languages and music could be heard, a Bible could be seen up close, scores of people could kneel quietly before an ornate shrine of a saint credited with miraculous healings. In some places huge buildings or caves made holy by a former resident could be visited, with hand-wrought tokens left by other pilgrims carefully placed around the sacred site. Some pilgrims had traveled very little, and were impressed by the largeness of their own countries.

Understandably, personal reactions to the actual experience of being at a shrine were very different from feelings about everyday routines in more familiar settings. New and surprising revelations came to mind, suggesting while still on journey that the future is already affecting the present. As pilgrims traveled farther and farther away from their homes and familiar routines to different scenes and cultures, they encountered new views of reality and could reappraise their lives with perspectives born of confronting newness "out there." Reality proved to be bigger than any one person's perception of it. Overall, it was as if they had stepped out of one world into another, into totally unexpected new possibilities.

Popular shrines often lived up to their name, which comes from the Latin word *scrinium,* meaning receptacle or box for a treasured item, perhaps a saint's relic. For pilgrims, the treasure could be something both longed for and mysterious, which would be waiting there just for them. Sometimes even the sense of value itself came suddenly, both intensely and unexpectedly.

As I consider the experiences reported by pilgrims from the distant past, I also recall my first significant adult journey which, I realized after long consideration, was itself a pilgrimage. Curiously, my journey was not a search for new sites or sights, but instead a return to settings intimately familiar much earlier in my life. What began as a sentimental journey, or perhaps an effort to escape pain, proved to be far more.

My situation was one of grief and confusion. When alone I yearned for the company of others, yet after a short time in a chatty group I wanted to flee from it and be on my own. This pattern could occur several times a day. The harsh reality was bereavement, for I had been widowed some nine months previously and after Alice's death my home seemed desolate to me even with the support of an affectionate son and daughter and a lively circle of friends. I could pour energy into my work, and did so almost automatically. In truth, the work was too intense for what I needed far more—a lessened pace that allowed nurture for my reflective side. Constant busyness probably delayed the admission of mourning and its integration into my ongoing life.

Urged by my superior at work to take my vacation during the less busy summer period, I chose to spend about a week at each of three places important to my growing up and in our early marriage. That decision led me back to three states: Kentucky, Virginia, and Maryland. More important, as it turned out, was my harkening to the counsel I had given others over the years: to face into the painful process of mourning, rather than trying to deny or escape it. If I could endure passage through the difficult period, I might find a new sense of peacefulness.

Looking toward my childhood roots, I went first to Kentucky where I spent several days with family members and walked well-remembered streets. To my dismay, several sites prominent in my memories had long since disappeared. A parched, empty lot gave no hint that the solid brick building of my first school had once stood there. Still more disconcerting, a large island in the Ohio River, once a midpoint resting place for canoe trips, had also vanished as the water level rose after a navigational lock was constructed downstream. I drove and walked to places I wanted to revisit. I was able to speak and hear words of consolation with cherished people, but I did not find what might fill the void within me.

Reconnecting with my son and his family continued the healing process, though no magical change became evident while among the rolling Virginia hills. My impression a few years ago was that not much happened during this portion of my journey. But I had forgotten! The journal I kept on this pilgrimage reminds me that instead of feeling the pain begin to disappear, I initially felt it increase. This was my first extended vacation trip without my late wife. Observing the lives of our son and his family, I relived parts of my own busy activities of work, church involvement, raising children, and much more—but I was sad that their mother and grandmother Alice could not also be enjoying them. My journal reminds me of another very important shift: that my own offspring had begun to accept me as a single person, and valued me in that new state. They had, in fact, made an adjustment I myself had not yet achieved.

The following week in Maryland I encountered a number of people, settings, and memories most directly bound to my life with Alice. As I shared with her mother and sisters in their mourning, restorative health was quietly working within me. My reentry into the scenes and memories of my former life was difficult, especially on one railway station platform where I remembered the surge of joy I had felt there decades earlier on spotting my bride-to-be running down a similar platform to welcome me back from the war. On my sentimental journey, I was aware that for some minutes the grimy windows of the train had so diffused the early morning sunlight that I was unable to see a thing beyond the car. Only now do I perceive that my outlook about the future had also seemed impenetrable.

An immense change took place within the span of one week in Annapolis. On the morning of my departure, I felt I had been raised to such a comforting new level of awareness that I said to our daughter later in California that the aircraft really had not needed wings, for I could have provided the necessary uplift.

So hope for a lessening of my grief did come at the end of the three weeks of travel—not as a quick shift like the turning of a switch, but in a haunting image that remained with me for weeks. It came early one morning soon after my return, when I chose to meditate for a period of time rather than to jog along the beach still in my east coast time frame. The vivid image came quickly, as my journal records:

> I am a jumble of thoughts and feelings! The image which came to mind at the very beginning of this day was the mouth of a river down which a great amount of water flowed swiftly, carrying with it whole trees and soil and general clutter—but no boats in the tan-color liquid rush. Why all of the litter should remain at the *mouth* of the river is a big mystery. Why did it not flow on into the sea? Obviously [a word that came too easily!], because something is restraining, is "refusing" to let the flow be complete. That is exactly the way I feel. There has been a mighty flow within me. The image tells me that it is all "natural" debris, matter just awaiting a cleansing flood. Moreover, there

are no live trees within the jam, no living shrubs—all matter which was dead before the flood began.

It is a cleansing flood, as I contemplate the movement, not a destructive deluge. But there is power, and this power waits to be released. I feel the need for direction—no, help! And I am thinking this is the shape of the future—weeks, I trust, but it terrifies me to contemplate years, for a personal longing of great intensity is mixed intimately with all the clutter—and the awakening of such deep feelings both terrifies me and gives me a future filled with hope.

Some guidance and clarification of my meditation experience came soon afterward, during a luncheon conversation in which I related the details of this image of a river to a friend. He softly inquired, "As you viewed the flood, Doug, were you looking upstream or downstream?" I realized immediately that I had been looking upstream, toward the past, rather than downstream toward the future—an unknown future I feared might have oceanic proportions and involve my loss of control.

Several years passed before I began to sense a connection among several key elements: Alice's death, my travel to people and scenes important in my past, a dramatic image of rushing water, and the realization that new possibilities accompanied my loss. I now add a further element: that healing and pilgrimage quite naturally fit together. I realize also that several deep reasons for my journey were not near enough to the threshold of awareness for me to recognize them at the time. I had, in truth, traveled not merely for diversion and escape, but to validate myself as the same person I had known for years, although still missing the most important person in my life. I had been searching to reclaim my identity, along with a restored sense of well-being, but I first needed the catharsis of mourning.

I can now laugh about my hasty reaction to the brief glimpse I had of a bird shortly after Alice's death, when I was driving to the monastery we had visited many times over the years. Part of the way up a mountain pass, I spotted a hawk high on a branch of a solitary dead tree alongside the highway. The hawk was hunkered down, facing into the lively wind. "Silly creature," I thought while driving past, "why don't you face in the other direction?" Today I know that such a shift would not have calmed the wind, but merely ruffled the bird's feathers. Whether the bird squinted its eyes against the wind or made other adjustments, I shall never know; but I do realize that my facing into the reality of loss had helped me accept an unknown future. The unsettling elements of my trip were gracefully accompanied by a sense of emptying that made room for healing, though more than a year would pass before I could comfortably recite with Psalm 30, "You have turned my mourning into dancing" (v. 11).

Because of this experience and this journey, I can identify with the many thousands of people who visit shrines in search of healing. Though hesitant about entering into debate about what actually takes places at these sites, I am impressed by the commitment of pilgrims I have seen at shrines like Holywell, in Wales. Early during my first visit there, admittedly for sightseeing, I observed what occurred after two buses unloaded a large group of visitors of obviously serious intent. All gathered in the sunlight around a musician at a keyboard. After several hymns and prayers, interspersed with periods of silence, several of the group assisted someone in a wheelchair into the still water of the expansive pool nearby. Others waded in the pool at shallow locations, or scooped up water to pour over their forearms or to mark their foreheads. Their actions repeated what countless others have done there over a period of thirteen hundred years.

Religious shrines are venerated and visited regularly in countries throughout the world—they are one of the most enduring influences in religious traditions. These holy places are mountains, such as Kilimanjaro in Tanzania or Denali ("the great one" to the aboriginal residents) in Alaska, or rivers, caves, and stones. Sometimes the gathering spots are beneath trees at high places, such as the oaks at Shechem where God appeared to Abraham, where Jacob buried foreign idols, and where Joshua assembled the tribes after initial success in the conquest of Canaan. A majority of these healing shrines are accessible water sources, notably wells and springs.

The focal point for Holywell is the spring, which flows from a spot below the village into a creek bed and thence to the estuary where the River Dee joins the Irish Sea. The water's run down a steep incline is about two miles, at a rate once measured at almost five hundred gallons per minute. A chapel was built long ago over the spring's precipitous site, one side resting on earth and the other three sides on high pillars. Many years ago a score of factories operated mills downstream of this vigorous water source, but now a busy highway passes alongside the revered scene.

Why is the shrine at Holywell so popular, and why was it permitted to continue as a pilgrimage shrine during periods when monasteries and other holy places were being destroyed? Convincing responses to those questions are no easier than answers to the question of what really happens when people come for healing. But several threads are evidently woven into popular beliefs about Holywell's shrine. First there is the tale of Winifred, a seventh-century woman of great beauty who was slain by a lustful tribal prince when she refused his overtures, but soon revived when her severed head was rejoined by the ministration of St. Beuno, her uncle and the abbot of a monastic community. Legend says that the water burst forth from this site at the moment of the miracle. It is not surprising, then, that people have sought healing in those waters, and the emerging shrine was visited by more people in search of physical healing than for penance or devotion.

A second thread is more ancient. It dates from a few years before Winifred's legendary healing in advice given by Pope Gregory the Great to Augustine and his missionary monks at Canterbury. Pope Gregory suggested that the missionaries not eradicate old beliefs by force, but rather accept those beliefs that were compatible with Christianity and turn them to good account. A pagan temple was not destroyed, for example, but became one of the initial abbey structures. Thus the missionaries did not use force, which would meet with resistance, but softened and converted by examples of a gentler life.

The third and perhaps most significant thread in the story of Holywell applies also to other shrines: namely, the powerful symbolic nature of water. Water is not only necessary for life, it is the major means of cleansing, both physical and spiritual. It surrounds and nourishes babies before they are born. Water is central to many sacred rituals, of which baptism is but one. In our day water is a symbol for the subconscious. For centuries it has symbolized God's power to give life and to refresh. Wells that were originally sacred sites of paganism acquired Christian overtones: "So the well of which the spring came mysteriously from the underworld and was guarded by a numinous woman with the power to heal became a place for Christian pilgrimage."[1]

The famed shrine of Lourdes in southwestern France is of much more recent origin than Holywell, and has been the focus of much discussion in medical and theological circles. In 1858 a fourteen-year-old girl named Bernadette Soubirous reported several visions and conversations with the Blessed Virgin Mary, at which time a spring had appeared in a grotto of rock. Miraculous healings were soon reported, and pilgrims flocked to the site. In time a huge church was built near the grotto, and sightseers thronged there among the continuing flow of pilgrims. Visitors continue to visit Lourdes, although its record of genuine healings has been questioned by some. In a book written in the sixties, Alan Neame stated that fewer than one hundred cures were authenticated in a period of more than one hundred and twenty years. He noted, however, that the statistics concentrated on physical healing but ignored all forms of mental illness, as well as the emotional side of physical illness. After interviewing many pilgrims, the author concluded that "the majority of sick pilgrims who go to Lourdes return home saying that they feel better (even though they recognize that they are not

---

1. D. J. Hall, *English Medieval Pilgrimage* (London: Routledge & Kegan Paul, 1965), 24.

cured). This feeling-better is variously ascribed to divine grace, human fellowship, the lovely change and the effort of will."[2]

Religious shrines and vacation spas have a number of things in common, among which are the support of like-minded companions and time away from home. The paths of tourists and pilgrims to water sites crossed during the eighteenth and nineteenth centuries at popular spas such as Bath in southwestern England, where many "took the waters." In many popular resort settings these were mineral waters, some carbonated and some not, issuing forth at many locations in Europe and America. Patrons were enthusiastic about the results, though chemical analyses could not always show a significant difference between the waters of the spa and those back home. But the visitors were away from normal irritants and enjoying a different climate, lifestyle, and diet. There were fascinating diversions, and new things to think about; cheerful people and the experience of relaxation and fresh air. In any case, for many the trips were indeed occasions of renewal and healing.

ॐ

My journey into the past was certainly not an ordinary trip, and although I did not visit a shrine where healings had taken place or "take the waters" of any fresh springs, in retrospect I believe a healing pilgrimage is an apt name for the experience. As I seek to recount in simple terms what took place during that trip, I

---

2. Alan Neame, *The Happening at Lourdes: The Sociology of the Grotto* (New York: Simon and Schuster, 1967), 171.

recollect that I was primarily not trying to forget a treasured relationship, but seeking relief from persistent pain. On the surface, my movement from place to place was simply exposing myself to persons and places from my past. But the places were real places, as in time my adjustment would be to a new reality and not to an imagined future. Perhaps even more important was my taking time for meditation and reflection on my encounters, both in thinking about them at the time and in writing about my experiences afterward. Later I realized that I was moving from the distant past to the near past, and from there into the real present. At the same time, I was seeking the possibility of something new.

Only when I was on the way home from Maryland, realizing I had completed my planned itinerary, did I sense that something important had taken place in my three weeks away from home. I had no idea of the details, but I felt as if I had passed through a gateway or stepped over an important threshold. Later I recollected a scene from C. S. Lewis's book *The Last Battle,* the seventh and final volume of the *Chronicles of Narnia*. There is a strange doorway in the story, not magic in itself but a sort of test of reality. Out in open space stands a door and its frame—nothing else, with no building or other structure around it. A skeptical young prince walks around the unusual object, verifying that it is a door and frame when viewed from either side. But his friend assures him that to look through a crack between two planks forming the door is infinitely different, as indeed to walk through it is also. And to pass through it—to *choose* to cross the threshold—is to discover that "its inside is bigger than its outside." That was my experience at the completion of my eastward journey, and I am convinced is often a perception gained from true pilgrimage.

As noted earlier, anthropologists Victor and Edith Turner have likened pilgrimage experiences to crossing thresholds. Such was my experience on the sentimental journey long before I was aware of their writing: I was passing from one state of mind and being into another. An additional image—also in the metaphor of a building—has come to me: that of a window into new possibilities. As a sacred or sentimental journey can expose a traveler to new views of the world and of society, so it can give new views into oneself that extend beyond the present to the future.

⚭

Questions for Reflection

Can you recall a journey that gave you a deep sense of healing and rest after your travel was completed? What aspects of that journey were significant to you?

Recall an important reunion with people or with a place. How quickly were you able to "reconnect"? What facilitated that reunion? What changes to the people or place surprised you?

What are your thoughts about shrines acclaimed for their physical healing properties? Do you believe the recovery of emotional or relational ease is valid healing?

To what extent does water have symbolic meaning to you? In what ways?

Victor and Edith Turner have written that pilgrimage often involves passing over a threshold to newness. How do you relate to that image? Is the concept of a window into new life possibilities helpful in your view of pilgrimage?

Shaping a Pilgrimage

As a form of prayer, the pilgrimage is an incarnational
prayer, a prayer of the body. The pilgrim is a person
who prays with his feet.

Edward Hays

Given the different ideas of what pilgrimage is, I
hesitate to offer specific guidelines about how to
incorporate a pilgrim view into recreational travel.
Some travelers will resist the insertion of serious
planning into the pleasures of exploring new places and
scenes: "I'm here for fun, not analysis!" And why add to
all the information already offered? Travel guides and
memoirs often draw on a whole range of insights from
historians, anthropologists, scientists, geographers,
and poets, giving readers a sense of recapturing the
essence of childhood or moving into new feelings of
hopefulness about the rest of life in the same way a
pilgrimage can. Pleasing surprises often come
unplanned, however, and I have accompanied some
travelers who commented on unexpected changes that
took place within themselves while on a trip intended to
explore certain things "out there."

Having said this, I now propose eight key elements
that shape a pilgrimage. They can help you to reflect

more deeply on your travel and perhaps you will realize for the first time that pilgrimage is for seeing the present as well as for looking into the past, and for yourself as well as for others. We cannot easily avoid stereotypes in our thinking about travel. Each trip-taker's judgment will be partially shaped by centuries-old views about pilgrimage, but also by possibilities that did not even exist a century ago.

My hope in writing this chapter is to help the traveler reach a deeper valuing of the journey that is possible when a periodic "taking stock" accompanies our physical movement. Reflection during a journey can greatly enrich the experience, as can detailed advance planning. Pilgrimage is not limited to the present moment; as I have said, our past views shape our expectations, while our ongoing lives set the course for our future outlook.

&co: *Quest*

The first and basic mark of pilgrimage is the quest for something personally important enough to motivate a committed search. The quest is significant because it is shaped largely by our conviction that a proposed trip promises an outcome for which we have yearned, and which merits the exertion necessary to proceed. Thus an element of trust or hopefulness is an important motivator, a companion to the desire that prompts our movement. Moving *toward* a goal, furthermore, is usually more creative than a journey that is an attempt to escape from something.

But for what might a pilgrim search? What is a common objective of a quest? Often the quest is for something that we sense is missing, or that seems like a good sequel to some past experience, or perhaps the glimpse of a new basis for reshaping life itself. Nor are these prompting forces confined to individuals. Social changes over the years are an influence, for example. The perceived loss of a national way of life—"the good old days"—attracts crowds to certain settings, such as the battlefields of the Revolutionary War or the historical reconstructions of Williamsburg and Jamestown. Belief that old ways should be known and honored has fostered the creation of state landmarks and commercial theme parks alike. Entertainment in the nostalgic vein constitutes a major industry in America.

The desire for wholeness (akin to "holiness" in scripture) draws us toward certain places rather than to others, leading us to new places instead of staying at home. Thus the quest for holy places continues as pilgrims are attracted to the shrines of the past. The search may be an effort to repair what has been broken: health, freedom, an important relationship, family or communal harmony, or a vague, lost dream about how life might someday be. I suspect that more often the search is to regain what has been lost suddenly by tragedy or gradually by a slipping away over time. Frequently the death of an important person hastens the decision to begin a quest. A loved one has departed; perhaps I should search elsewhere in my life as well. Or increased sensitivity to the swift passage of time can lead one forth to experience something specific "before it's too late."

Sometimes I am startled to realize that something I formerly valued has disappeared from my thoughts, or that a once important relationship seems to have faded. Now and again I think about the parable of the lost sheep in Luke's gospel and wonder if I do not become lost in much the same way. The sheep of Jesus' parable probably became lost gradually, munching their way from one clump of grass to the next, unaware that they were slowly moving away from the rest of the flock. So life's succession of involvements leads me away from a sense of security and wholeness I once took for granted.

Although it is somewhat more abstract, surely a powerful motivation for travel and quest over the centuries is the search for a center around which we can reorganize our life. During those times in history when Chaos and Fate seemed to be in control, people longed for a transcendent center, a God who would bring about order and safety. Shrines were dedicated to saints, who presumably could approach God on behalf of the pilgrim. At the present time, with technology so influential in decision-making, we can feel under assault by the rapidity of change. Because complexity dominates, our search for simplicity takes on urgency in many of our lives, a way to bypass the confusion.

Summarizing the first and fundamental mark of pilgrimage, a quest is an active search born of deep longing and trust that one's desire will be honored at the end of the seeking.

ଓଓ *Place*

Wandering *can* lead to pilgrimage, but a specific focus is more helpful. Therefore I suggest that a second key element of pilgrimage is *an attainable physical site* toward which the quest is directed. Whether it is the mystical attraction of the place or one's own heightened sense of spiritual awareness, pilgrimage involves specific places and people, living or dead. Just as real life is always situated in time and space, so is real pilgrimage. Choosing a physical focus—a site to visit—

is a helpful beginning in the search for a new center or expanded boundary within which life may be lived.

Before and during the Middle Ages, shrines were established soon after the death of some charismatic figure around whom a cult of devotion had formed. The same is true today, though the shrines may be very different from traditional holy places. The faithful visitations of a few devotees can be sufficient attraction for newcomers; if great numbers of people visit a particular spot, others will want to do likewise. The mystical attraction of a popular place builds rapidly, and not necessarily in ways that are open to explanation. In contrast to the centuries-long search for the Holy Grail, today's devotion is as mobile as modern forms of travel. In view of this reality, I suggest that a prospective pilgrim follow her urge to visit a place that claims her heart, while still being attentive to the other key elements I am now going to propose.

෨෨ *Movement*

Pilgrims cannot reach the objectives of their quests without *physical movement*, an obvious third element. One must bestir oneself. Pilgrimage is participation, not a spectator activity, and it is much deeper than entertainment. In the past pilgrimage was viewed as "prayers of the feet." Today's movement may involve several kinds of transportation, though I cling to the conviction that the experience will be more valued if substantial exertion is involved.

Ironically, one of the reasons for the breakdown of church-imposed medieval pilgrimages was that it became possible for one's offenses to be pardoned almost effortlessly, by proxy, as more and more "professional" pilgrims did the actual journeying for penitents who remained at home. The pardoner in Chaucer's *Canterbury Tales* reminds us that as mercenary soldiers could be paid to fulfill another's military duties, so people paid proxies to go on pilgrimage for them. Perusal of today's newsstands reveals the modern fantasy that we can live our lives through a heroine or hero of the moment: the outright projection of our hopeful fantasies onto other people. The physical exertions of pilgrimage take on an increased importance today as a way of countering passivity: pilgrimage involves us directly in a quest that is already important to us.

෨෨ *Planning*

While not advocating that your travel be grueling, I do recommend that if you are hoping to go on pilgrimage you live for some time with the urge to journey before setting forth. That way, you can invest yourself in the enterprise by imagining the journey ahead of time and learning as much about where you are going as you can. Perhaps you will then be better able to perceive the interior call as a true yearning and not simply one more in a succession of whims.

Detailed planning, a fourth element in pilgrimage, will help this conviction take shape and also build excitement about the upcoming journey. I find it helpful to recall that the slow approach to medieval shrines must have brought with it increased anticipation. How thrilling it must have been to walk over a rise on a roadway and behold a massive cathedral larger than one's entire home village—sometimes painted in gay colors rather than the gray stonework evident today! Not only did the prospect of soon reaching the goal raise a traveler's spirits, but so did nearby wayside chapels, along with musical, magical, and gymnastic entertainment only dreamed about at home, souvenir stands, and other attractions situated on the major routes to the more popular shrines. I imagine that these entertainments were as full of drama as the shrines themselves, and recollected just as often in the months and years to come.

A journey can acquire the qualities of pilgrimage most readily when it is not rushed, when you do your own pre-journey preparation, and especially when your advance planning anticipates in detail all that you will encounter. Childlike expectancy heightens receptivity, as knowing some details quickens the later sense of identifying with the site. Many pilgrims want to touch the objects about which they have heard and read, letting what was imagined perhaps months earlier become real and physically within reach. Another common impulse is to remain silent in the presence of the achieved goal: "I have longed to be here—and now I'm here!"

∞ *Time*

Time, or perhaps *timing,* is a fifth important element of pilgrimage—and a many-faceted element it is. Calendar dates may control the period when you can be away from other responsibilities, just as they may also set the optimum period for arrival at certain shrines. The season of Lent or high feast days are significant for Christian pilgrims, as are Passover and the Feast of Tabernacles for Jews. The major Muslim pilgrimage *(hajj)* begins on the eighth of Dhu al-Hijjah. Travelers at such times can be assured of sharing the company of similarly minded people, sometimes thousands competing for accommodations and ease of movement, a ferment that can work for good or ill depending on how you look at it.

Apart from the calendar, sufficient time should be allowed for you to feel as well as see the ambiance of a pilgrim site, and to reflect upon its impact on other people since its beginning. Quiet periods to meditate at odd moments throughout the day give meaning to the pilgrimage while it is still in process. If I can see and imagine a setting or object as if from within itself, the impact of the meeting can be integrated within myself. "What was special about this saint? Wasn't she a lot like others I have known—perhaps struggled in life as I have? In what ways does her life influence my life? Why am I here among these hundreds of visitors? Will I feel the same when I return home? Can I take some of my healing back to others?" Thereby I can be aware of a private, often deep inner meaning I would not otherwise know. Thus I rate the inner meditative journey as equal in importance to the physical movement of my journey or the attainment of a physical objective. Better yet is the combination of outward and inner seeking—and both require time.

Still another significant sort of time is *timeliness*. We must take into account what is happening in our own lives and in the world about us. What waits for us at the goal is not neatly separable from what we bring as either uplift or burden to the place. Borrowing from Emerson's opinion that good readers make good books, I believe that good pilgrims make good pilgrimages. What you find at a chosen site depends largely upon what you take with yourself to that site. One traveler may comment, "It was just what I needed at this time of wondering what my life is really about." Or another may confess, "I guess I have not been ready and receptive until now. The timing seems perfect this year."

꙳ *Companionship*

A sixth important element of pilgrimage is your *interaction with fellow pilgrims,* although this is a suggestion I offer with some caution. Openness to sharing the experience with others can greatly enrich your appreciation of a visited site, and fellow travelers can point out details that you might easily miss. You will have others on hand to share your own excitement on discovering the different aspects of a pilgrimage site.

But total immersion in a group may also deprive you of the opportunity for rich introspection. Generous amounts of both community and private reflection offer not simply a compromise, but a choice that can bring an enduring richness long after fellow travelers have gone their separate ways. Medieval pilgrim bands have been described as people who came together through a focus on their ultimate goal, not because of things they might have had in common in their home settings. I suspect that the traveler who must constantly refer to "back home" has not fully entered the process of true pilgrimage.

꙳ *Identity*

Interaction with others reminds me of the seventh element of pilgrimage, which is openness to *seeing oneself as a pilgrim.* This element is as complex as any I suggested earlier, for it involves a willingness to prepare oneself seriously, to listen before jumping to conclusions, to consider the merits of points of view you may not have previously considered, and to appreciate the circumstances in the past that first led to a particular site's adoption as a pilgrimage shrine. The more you seek to identify with such differences, the more your perspective can grow and the more you can appreciate the element of timelessness in the adventure of pilgrimage—extending beyond the interval of travel.

⊗⊗ *Awe*

In this listing of basic elements of pilgrimage, I reserve for my eighth and final suggestion the importance of treating the visited place with *reverence*. A tourist might respect the religious practices observed by others at the site; a pilgrim should always do so. Disrespect diminishes a shrine's sacred nature, whereas a quiet presence honors what is precious. Some pilgrim visitors might offer prayers, or join a religious observance taking place at the time. At the very least, a quiet appreciation can be offered; your attitude can be as important as any outward gestures. These regulations posted at Lourdes, for example, might seem constraining to tourists, but have certainly been valued by other travelers who are visiting the shrine for healing:

> Pilgrims in the Domain of Our Lady
> be decently dressed.
> Gentlemen: legs and arms covered.
> Ladies: wear a dress, head and arms covered.
> Sport clothes are not suitable for a pilgrimage.
> Do not smoke. Remember where you are.
> Absolute silence in the churches,
> in the grotto, in the baths.

৩৫

Now and again I fantasize how any pilgrimage would be "at its best," while still unclear what I mean by it. I feel strongly that pilgrimage should be utterly personal irrespective of whether I am traveling with a group or alone. If a seemingly ordinary experience remains with me, that is likely so because I have truly attempted to become part of the place, the people, the season of the year, or whatever else I remember vividly. There would have been at least one significant focal point; my movements would have been more than simple wandering. Altogether, I might feel that I had crossed some boundary or threshold—or that I was privileged to look through a new window onto life, and life would be different because of the experience. As the years pass, I would probably look back on the journey as a sacred holiday and realize I had received a gift, perhaps in part because I was receptive to the possibility of grace: I was an attentive pilgrim rather than a casual visitor.

Movement, I imagine, would not cease at my journey's end, for I would carry with me a sense of moving on in life itself. I would have a fresh view of my own identity and worth, and perhaps even experience new health and well-being. My original intent to visit a place associated with a person or way of life I had honored would add to some important perceptions about myself; they might even urge me on to further internal work somewhat freer of narcissism because I had discovered a comfort in simply being myself in a very mixed group. Traveling begun with apprehension might have swept away old burdens and concerns, and made room for new explorations and assessments. Taking a few steps back from my fantasy in order to make some generalizations, I might conclude that a real pilgrimage allows significant personal transformation. Because the change is internal, it will accompany me long after the geographical journey has ended. A play on two similar long words comes to mind. Because I have ventured to new boundaries in places, companionship, and personal inquiry—moved out to a new *perimeter*—I will be conscious of new *parameters*: principles and measurable dimensions that will continue to inform my life. I will hold within my grasp some new thing I can monitor and evaluate for the ongoing enrichment of my life. Boundaries that I might have used for my own protection in the past can prove to be the thresholds of new openings.

ଔଔ

Questions for Reflection

Pilgrimages have been called "prayers of the feet," implying that physical movement is necessary. What suggestions can you offer to a person who longs to go on pilgrimage but who cannot travel or is unable to leave important commitments at the moment?

The author comments that the sheep of Jesus' parable probably got lost gradually. Can you recollect something about your life which has drifted away without your being aware of it? Could a specially planned journey help you to reclaim what is lost?

"The time was just right for this," is a comment often voiced by pilgrims. Recall similar feelings you have experienced on one or more trips. What made the time "right"?

In your actions, do you prefer to believe that you are moving away from the known or moving toward the unknown?

Chapter Eight

Pilgrims Together: A Benedictine Fortnight

It is a blessed thing to have fellow travelers to the New
Jerusalem. If you cannot find any you must make them,
for none can travel the road alone.

John Wesley

A soft voice whispered in my ear, "The coach is here."
Leaving my bowl of oatmeal porridge on the
breakfast table, I hastened to greet the newly arriving
guests outside the front entrance of St. Deiniol's
Library. A few of the dozen travelers seemed alert, the
rest sleepy after their overnight flight from America and
an hour's minibus ride from Manchester Airport. Most
of the newcomers gazed wonderingly at the imposing
sandstone building and its large oak door. A few helped
the driver unload bags soon to be unpacked and not
needed again for two weeks. Then began a brief
confusion of locating rooms, carrying luggage, and
deciding whether to eat or sleep, or possibly explore the
grounds of the library. Few of the group knew each
other, or the additional twelve participants arriving
later in the day, but that would change quickly as the
Benedictine Fortnight, as we called this experience,

began to unfold. And although I was not the provider of room and board, I fancied myself as the innkeeper in Chaucer's *Canterbury Tales* who became so interested in his guests' pilgrimage to the shrine of St. Thomas that he joined them on their way!

I want to use the example of this Benedictine Fortnight to offer some detailed insights into the kind of background planning necessary for a two-week group experience of pilgrimage. It will follow the same order of the eight key elements suggested in the preceding chapter: the idea of quest, the physical site, travel, prior planning, questions of time, getting along with fellow travelers, viewing oneself as a pilgrim, and reverence for visited sites.

Our shared pilgrimage was not to a single shrine. Rather, the quest was more thematic and internal: to explore the history and ongoing wisdom of the Benedictine way of life as it might pertain to our lives today. On the surface, we might have appeared mainly to visit places illustrating how one strand of monasticism evolved: from a seventh-century hermit's cell to small and large abbey ruins, and from viable monastic communities to vibrant cathedral-abbeys of recent origin. But the rhythm we observed during our stay at St. Deiniol's Library added a second dimension and helped our internal quests to take shape: a routine of worship, meals, lectures, informal gatherings, group study, recreation, and free time for study and reflection or for travel in the vicinity. These activities and trips richly complemented each other, but the depth of search was ultimately an individual matter to the extent that each participant chose to be involved.

Why the Benedictine theme? Primarily, Norvene and I had been involved in related study and experiments with that lifestyle at home, had already conducted workshops and retreats on the subject, and were encouraged by others who wanted to join us on a group exploration abroad. People we knew had expressed interest in living a balanced way involving body, mind, and spirit—faithful to daily prayer, study, and work. Several people wanted to spend two weeks with others willing to share their successes and failures in past attempts to apply monastic insights to their own lives "in the world."

Our choice of a Benedictine theme also reflects a growing interest in society at large, notably the success of recent books on several strands of Christian spirituality and specifically monastic life, musical recordings of Gregorian chant, and a resurgence in the popularity of retreat centers. We suspected that former churchgoers who had briefly searched for meaning in the great eastern religions often did not make lasting connections there, and were now ready to explore more deeply the insights of their own western spiritual roots. Most likely the ongoing search was not to replace but rather to complement regular church involvement with something demanding a deeper personal commitment. Altogether, the time seemed right to find others to accompany us on pilgrimage.

On our shared quest, the group soon realized that all of us wanted to walk about sites of which we had heard, and to touch and savor the sensations evoked by those settings, just as Egeria had longed to do in the fourth century and countless pilgrims have both before and since. The preferred sites were associated with people we admired—Aelred of Rievaulx and his sensitive writing about friendship; Cuthbert of Durham, who continued to live with the poor after he became a bishop; Winifred of Holywell, who survived a seemingly mortal wound to minister to her people for many years. Tiny St. Asaph's Cathedral in North Wales was special to us because the Bible was translated into Welsh there. Immense Coventry Cathedral reminded me that wartime fire bombing of the previous cathedral did not engender continuing hatred, but rather initiated a continuing commitment to reconciliation. I recall more than once thinking at places I had long heard about, "I am here where so-and-so made her/his impact on humankind—and that matters to me." Significantly, I was with fellow pilgrims who also cared, and their commitment further validated my own quest.

We wanted to visit authentic sites, places where real historical events occurred. Nearby Chester was a convenient place from which to launch our visit of Benedictine sites. We first visited the cathedral there as a group when the cathedral staff was preparing to celebrate the nine-hundredth anniversary of its foundation as a Benedictine community. We were invited to sit in the cathedral choir as the monks would have done, gathering for worship over many years until their community was dissolved by Henry VIII in the early sixteenth century. In our separate ornately carved choir stalls, we were all the more aware of holiday visitors sitting some distance from us in the large nave, where townspeople would have gathered for centuries in quiet witness to the monks' several daily offerings of prayer and chanting. Cathedral guides pointed out to us a line of cement in the wall where Gothic style joined the older Norman architecture: an apt symbol for our own hope of bringing together an ancient lifestyle with our own varied lives today.

Two days later we journeyed southward to Valle Crucis Abbey. In contrast with Chester, where passing centuries and urban crowding jointly conspired to erase the evidence of monastic buildings once framing the dominant cathedral structure, the rural setting of Valle Crucis helped us to visualize the daily life of two or three dozen men there at the beginning of the thirteenth century. We speculated about their worship, food preparation, clothing, sanitation, and labor in the fields. Several of our number voiced the wish that they could find such peace at home, while others commented on the cool and drizzly summer day, wondering how many times a day they would have been allowed to thaw out in the single warming room during winter seasons. Group sentiment seemed solidly against daily 2 A.M. rising for worship, and all rejoiced in the virtual absence of visitors to the seemingly remote site only two miles from bustling Llangollen.

About a week later, we visited the ruins of the much larger abbeys of Rievaulx and Fountains in Yorkshire, far to the northeast in England. On the evening and next morning of our only overnight stay away from the library, we joined the monks in the choir stalls of Ampleforth Abbey for Evensong, sung in Latin, and for Lauds next morning in English.

As a diversion for a group whose preferences we did not know in advance, we had also scheduled a northward trip to the Lake District of England—lovely indeed, but tiring for some people who later confided that they did not need to be entertained. Such candor helped us to shape future Fortnights. Meanwhile, we also learned that adherence to a central theme makes some long travel more acceptable. Several days later and well south of our home base, Coventry Cathedral reminded us that the city itself began as a Benedictine monastery, initially supported by Lady Godiva and her husband Leofric, Earl of Mercia. Before that excursion we had also visited one of the smallest cathedrals in Britain: St. Asaph's in northern Wales, where we were invited to conduct the service of Evensong.

"A great day, but it will be good to be home again!" was heard on several occasions as our bus drivers pulled out of the parking lots for return trips to St. Deiniol's Library. That quiet setting was the one stable place amidst our varied travel, assuring us of a hearty greeting, good care, and listening ears about our times away. As the days passed, all of us came to recognize the library as *home*, the place where "it all came together." Moreover there is something special about living in the same building with so many fine old books!

Chaucer's rhapsodic prologue to *The Canterbury Tales* notwithstanding—sweet showers, flowers, young sun, small birds who sleep through the night with one eye open to make their music—modern people want primarily to get "away" and get "there" expeditiously. But I am convinced that the optimum pilgrimage goal has to be sufficiently far away that one cannot make quick visits home to check on things. Separation from the usual routine is essential; hence distance is also. As noted earlier, I also believe that the pilgrim mood prospers when some exertion is involved. But personal energy levels vary, and not everyone wants to climb to the top of a castle tower simply because it is there. The equalizer for the Fortnights has been a sprinkling of free, unprogrammed periods when the more vigorous can venture out on their own and others can relax where they are.

☙☙

Fifteen months before our group settled in at St. Deiniol's, Norvene and I began to work with two senior librarians to plan details for the proposed pilgrimage. How intense would the Fortnight be? The general mood of St. Benedict's Rule itself provided helpful counsel: to offer a predictable structure announced in advance, with enough flexibility that minor changes could be made by group consensus. Basic to the plan was its focus on Benedictine spirituality, both historical background and modern relevance. Happily, a quick survey revealed a number of ancient and still active Benedictine and related Cistercian sites within easy driving distance from Hawarden. We would start with two half-day outings, then a couple of full-day trips, and one two-day trip to our most distant place in Yorkshire.

What else, other than travel, might we do? Three resources were at hand to enrich the alternating days at home. There were the rhythms already established at the library and Hawarden, such as chapel worship and meals and walking around the village. Norvene and I decided to offer at least twenty sessions of lectures and small group study, with some visiting speakers. And we knew we needed to provide free time for individuals to do as they wished. Everyone liked the rhythm of alternating days at home and days of travel. On a very practical level, we did not need to carry heavy luggage down early each morning to yet another bus and be on the road for a new destination; we were thankful not to reenact the movie *It's Tuesday, So It Must Be Belgium.*

Summarizing the planning element, three components were involved from the beginning: proposers, arrangers, and participants. As the proposers, my wife and I laid out the rationale, announced details of program and cost, and continued in contact with all participants after they had preregistered for the Fortnight. Our communications with the group included five mailings of details about travel, Benedictine history and practices, a reading list, a sampling of the Welsh language, and notes about current events in Great Britain. Additionally, anyone living near us gathered for a formal tea and conversation three months before the departure date. So far, most of the Fortnight participants have come from the United States, though a few have come from Canada, Europe, and Australia, and their ages have ranged from the twenties into the eighties.

In addition to our own efforts, we could draw upon the expertise and good humor of the library's subwarden, who arranged local travel and introductions to several communities, and handled many other details months ahead as well as during the Fortnight. We shared plans by letter and telephone on numerous occasions as the plan took final shape.

Individual planning beyond the details of travel can greatly enrich the experience: reading about places that will be visited, imagining and anticipating, "clearing the decks" at home before departure, even deciding how most smoothly to return home, with the inevitable chores and routines waiting for us. And what about timing? One-week and ten-day periods seemed too short, and a month was too long. Two weeks—a fortnight in British terms—had a good sound to it, and we settled on that length. When in the year? Suspecting that educators and church workers would constitute most of the group, we chose two weeks in August.

The interaction among fellow pilgrims is an important element of the experience. Usually, after three days together our pilgrim groups have taken shape. Prior to that, complaints of jet lag, fatigue, and a host of other issues cry out for tender loving care—if not damage control! Entries in my journal from the first few days of the initial Fortnight include: "A and B seem out of sorts with each other. C attends only some of the group offerings, as does D. E thrives on energetic exercise. F confides that she is not really accepted by the group, and seems withdrawn. G has suffered a migraine headache for three days. H is anxious to get back to his parish, though he has been away just a week. J nods off frequently. K vocalizes his objection to cold toast. L and M are fit to be tied that the electrical outlets do not jibe with their shaver, hair curler, or whatever."

Undoubtedly, I "bought into" concerns that I could not solve, and I sometimes felt like a buffer zone in the exchanges between our enlisted travelers and the established routines of the library. But there were many positive sentiments, beginning early with my journal note that "N rejoices that there are two left-hand writing surfaces on lecture room chairs" and multiplied in many notes given us at the end of the two weeks, including such glowing remarks as, "This is my best experience in the last twenty years or so."

Perhaps the liveliest meetings on each day spent at home were what we termed "chapter," named after old practices of English and Welsh monastic houses. Chapter refers to at least three things: place, participants, and purpose. Chapter houses are prominent in the consolidated layout of church and domestic buildings, often second only to the church in fine architectural details. Monks of medieval communities met daily as the chapter constituency to hear a chapter (or a portion) of their Rule read aloud, as well as to deal with work assignments for the day, communications needing the ear and voice of all, and individual confession of faults affecting community life.

Our chapter meetings deal with housekeeping matters that affect personal comfort and household routines, but they are not the place for discussion of lecture topics. In each meeting we set aside time for people to raise any questions they want. Early during the two weeks, inquiries are often about laundry facilities, unfamiliar electrical voltages and fixtures, and questions about "dos" and "don'ts" like, "Are we allowed to pick blackberries from the roadside hedges?" Some have shared their discoveries about the village, or insights from reading at their library carrels in spare moments; others have spoken about watching a group of seniors at lawn bowling down the highway, or magpies strutting across the croquet court adjacent to the building. Still others have announced that they would forgo a planned event in order to pursue a new interest, or to rest. By the second week, a more personal note emerges: "It's going just fine with me after a rocky start; thanks for putting up with my grumpiness," or, "I'm going into Chester this afternoon. Anyone want to go along? Can I pick up anything for anyone?"

Our Fortnights work best when everyone helps to shape the ongoing program. They may conduct chapel worship or serve as "coach coach" to assure that all hands are on board before a bus starts on its way. Seating at meals is by individual choice, as is participation in a skit night (respectfully termed "community play") at about the middle of the first week. The only activity in which all are asked to take part is our Bible meditation groups, in which we read scripture passages aloud and reflect upon them in groups of six or seven. These small groups clearly provide the deepest opportunity for bonding in both small clusters and the full group.

After five Benedictine Fortnights based at St. Deiniol's Library in Wales and two more recently held at Belmont Abbey in Hereford, England, our fellow pilgrims have consistently expressed their appreciation for the mixture of sightseeing with meditative exploring. Moreover, they say the previews we give of the sites to be visited the next day deepen their understanding of what could otherwise look like a jumble of stone. After that kind of careful preparation, we never hear comments similar to the one our nephew overheard from a young man to his wife at a Mayan site in Mexico: "See, I told you—just a pile of rocks!"

More extensive lectures also help to provide a mental framework for the overall theme of Benedictine pilgrimage. Popular topics include a survey of the religious history of England and Wales; some essential dynamics of community; the role of St. Benedict's Rule in monastic life; key women in British monasticism; learning to balance prayer, work, and study; *lectio divina,* a mode of reflective reading that shapes the heart as well as informs the mind and was the basis of our small group sessions; the ways Benedictine spirituality has adapted to the passage of the centuries; and the elements distinguishing pilgrimage from other kinds of travel.

Most of the pilgrims in our group also come to understand the relevance of the three Benedictine vows of stability, obedience, and *conversatio* to their everyday lives. *Conversatio* means a receptivity to personal transformation while remaining faithful to a well-regulated way of life. Granted that mobility is an essential element in our travels, the quieter, stabler periods at the library or abbey are valued as the times for integrating the many facets of sightseeing. A fresh view of obedience—a word that suggests deep listening and attentiveness to inward as well as outward messages—goes to its roots. Invariably, a large fraction of each group we have led share insights about how their lives might proceed in a less pressured fashion after our two weeks together. To me this validates the assumption that pilgrimage is a quest born of deep longing and trust that the desire will be honored at the end of the seeking.

ॐ

Evidently, many who take part in these Benedictine Fortnights consider their experience with us to be authentic pilgrimage. Most of them do not want the rush or the sense of regimentation that characterize commercial packaged tours. Some of them come from a sense of religious motivation, while others simply want to walk and stand where people they admire from earlier centuries have stood—it feels right to do so. It reminds me of the time I once stood near the shrine of Thomas à Becket in Canterbury Cathedral and tried to visualize how that quiet scene might have appeared in the thirteenth or fourteenth century when thousands streamed there with hopes of being healed. There would have been much noise, as some of the more energetic supplicants elbowed their ways for the closest possible approach—more insistent than reverent. What shape, I asked, might reverence take for me? I remained silent at that time, aware that the shrine had special meaning to countless others.

Later, at other shrines, I concluded that silence is helpful for pilgrims—or a simple docility that invites them to learn from what is before them. Keeping my tongue in check is more helpful, for example, than asking the guide whether a particular reliquary contains a splinter of the True Cross or how the skull of John the Baptist could possibly exist in three locations at once. In a group setting, therefore, I recommend that everyone focus their attention on one thing that attracts them at the site, whether a shrine, a cathedral, or a panoramic view of the River Wye Valley near the English-Welsh border. Observing silence in places where others have been at peace somehow bridges centuries of time. Group prayers echo the prayers offered by other gatherings at other times. The slow, solitary pacing of a cloister path follows the footsteps of others, and adds an active physical dimension to the mind's quiet reflection.

I am convinced that the pilgrim attitude offers real hope of discerning the sacred in the world around us. To remain silent while admiring the soaring arches of a ruined abbey can lead us to marvel at how such an immense structure could have been built five hundred years ago. Part of the answer lies in its skillful engineering and part in the conviction that it was built to the glory of God. Thus we can offer praise to God in a number of ways. In other places, an awareness of nature's splendor in a forest or in rolling waves at the seashore can, if we allow it, help us to know we are in the presence of God. Lack of reverence may be one of the elements that separates pilgrimage from sightseeing as a form of entertainment. In contrast, our respect validates the beauty of a site, and that can be our legacy to others who might also take the pilgrim path to the same place.

Our intentions and manner on entering a site largely shape the pilgrimage experience. Travelers looking for positive experiences will be more likely to find them, while the cynic will often reinforce a negative mindset. One does not find on pilgrimage more than one is willing to bring within oneself.

ॐ

Questions for Reflection

This chapter emphasizes focusing on a theme for pilgrimage, namely the Benedictine way of community life. What theme for a pilgrimage would appeal to you right now?

One aspect of pilgrimage is the practice of periodic reflection as a way of letting the experience become part of oneself. Does the discipline of meditation while traveling seem an intrusion to you?

Modern travel can transport people quickly to distant places. How do you think this access to quick travel affects our recreational sightseeing? pilgrimages?

At the moment, would you prefer to go on pilgrimage alone or in a group? Why?

What suggestions do you have for observing silence while visiting a busy pilgrimage site? Why do you think silence might be an important part of pilgrimage?

Fantasize that a substantial check and travel voucher arrive in your mail with a brief note: "We appreciate you greatly. The enclosed is for a trip of your choice. Be sure to come back to us. We love you!" After you have recovered from the surprise, how would you start to plan? What sort of trip would you choose? Where would you go?

᛭ᛞ᛭

Chapter Nine

On Pilgrimage Alone

We carry with us the wonders we seek without us.

Thomas Browne

G roup travel and firm scheduling are not everyone's preference. Sometimes we want to travel alone, or at most with one other person. We want the freedom to respond to opportunities as they arise on our journey, to set our own schedule and have time for reflection in solitude, and the fewer fellow-travelers our spontaneity will affect, the better it will be.

The world offers innumerable places to visit, yet few can meet all of our individual expectations. What suggestions can guide us when we are setting out alone? Probably the most helpful places, options, guidelines, and plans will be discovered and developed by the prospective pilgrims themselves, according to their interests and ability to travel. A strong and continuing desire to shape a pilgrimage in a distinctive way will probably be the essential element. When yearnings become strong enough, people begin to imagine and plan, to make decisions, and to counter fantasy with practicality.

In this chapter I shall briefly describe four journeys I have taken that were basically solitary, although they ended in the company of others. All had in common the fact that I had long yearned to undertake a specific trip, and that I judged each one in hindsight to have been a sacred journey. I had imagined years in advance that at least two of the four might be pilgrimages, rather than mere explorations, but I could only be sure later on. I now realize that all four exceeded my expectations, which had built during years of wondering, postponing, planning, and finally setting out.

My first example of solitary pilgrimage was a form of protest. I wanted to take action against what I considered excessive violence and injustice exerted by a major world power opposing a small nation in a devastating war. By the late 1960s I had concluded that the Vietnam War was unjust, but my cautious probing found few supportive hearts within the congregation that I served as pastor. After two or three years of meeting for affirmation with others of like mind, beyond my hometown, I learned that groups were forming to fly together from San Francisco and Los Angeles to Washington, D. C., where we could sit in passive resistance within the Capitol building. I immediately enlisted, informing only my immediate family, the parish lay leader, and another member of the congregation—and soon was on my way. I felt quite alone at the outset, but shortly recognized a few others at the airport, and by journey's end felt supported by a few hundred more on similar pilgrimages of protest.

I vividly recall a number of memorable aspects of this journey, now taken more than a quarter-century ago.

Soon after my return, I was called on to explain my actions, but the congregation and I survived the fallout and edged toward fresh dialogue at a level we had not encountered previously. From the moment of returning home, I have always considered this journey a most significant spiritual experience, one allowing me to remain faithful to the spirit of justice I had learned in my religious tradition. I especially valued the feeling of wholeness it gave me, whereas earlier I was internally divided—expressing my sentiments at home but unable to voice publicly what I really believed on several matters. That pilgrimage gave me fresh and personal insight into the well-known poem by Robert Frost:

> I shall be telling this with a sigh
> Somewhere ages and ages hence:
> Two roads diverged in a wood, and I—
> I took the one less traveled by,
> And that has made all the difference.

What began as a protest impelled by frustration and anger became a turning-point: I took the road less traveled. Nor did the transforming effects of my three-day pilgrimage end with myself. As members of the parish began to express their deeper thoughts and feelings as well, I felt less isolated. I was not evicted from their fellowship.

☙❧

My second solitary pilgrimage was a much-desired trip to the Holy Land. That journey fulfilled a long-held hope to walk where Jesus had walked and to experience the land that had been both cherished and fought over for millennia. The moment the plane touched down in Tel Aviv, I felt I had come home to my spiritual roots.

I offer this account of our visit to the Holy Land as an example of solitary pilgrimage, though I was in the company of perhaps two dozen others. But I had yearned so long to be there that I protected myself against all distractions. I had remained intentionally uninvolved in the planning of the trip before the group came together in Tel Aviv, and I was simply "soaking up" what was before me. I knew few details about this well-established tour in advance: a few of the sites we would be visiting, advice about clothes to pack, and precautions to exercise about health and passports. We did not know names of our fellow travelers in advance and even the guide was replaced just a few days before the tour began.

A sense of community built quickly among us as the enjoyable days passed. Just to share the same itinerary gave a common focus; we were committed as kindred seekers. Walking with others, hearing scripture together, and being aware of kneeling alongside one another added bit by bit to our sense of knowing each other more than we would have in attending the same church for several months. We "oohed" together about the beauty of rural Galilee, and one exclaimed in Tiberias that evening, "Can you believe that we're dancing the traditional *hora* on a porch right over the Sea of Galilee?"

Meanwhile, the tension in Jerusalem was palpable, with army tanks strategically situated and young male and female soldiers disposed in pairs about much of the city. We heard a woman arguing noisily about the price of zucchini at a sidewalk produce stand on the road we traversed along the Way of the Cross and I thought to myself, "Probably there was business as usual also on the day of crucifixion." On another occasion our bus driver, Joseph, became lost as he searched dark streets of Bethlehem. He admitted to those in the front seats, "Not only can't I find a room in the inn—I can't even find our inn!"

With so much activity and so many fellow travelers, how could this journey be a solitary one? Largely because, uncharacteristically, I remained on the fringes of the action, more in my thoughts and feelings. In my imagination I called up more Bible stories than the guides recalled at sacred sites, and resolved in advance to spend time apart from others for keeping my journal, prayer, and meditation. The full period of two weeks was a time for absorbing rather than informing, commenting, or comparing, though I certainly did some of each. A major shift was to a new understanding of my need for both apartness and togetherness with others. My times alone were often spent with my journal when group activities were not scheduled, or during early morning walks. There were many changes for quiet moments while simply standing a few feet apart from others before rejoining them. This was particularly helpful when we were in places where many other visitors were crowding to be near something special. However, whenever the group agreed to share an experience I became engaged—and even coauthored a farewell program for our pilgrim band.

ふの

I have described in some detail a third solitary trip to Iona in an earlier chapter. Now I simply add a brief assessment of why I went there, and why alone. My image of the visit is like a collage: fragments of very different shapes, colors, and textures that together form an artistic whole. I wanted to examine the vision I had shaped from the descriptions by many persons known and unknown to me. From my home setting in the complexity of a major city, I visualized Iona as continuing a simple way of life based in homey Celtic spirituality. How much had modern ways changed life there? I had heard that the post office was open only a couple of hours each weekday, and that a van brought banking service one day per week. What sort of terrain and plant life would I see on an island where summer weather is inviting but winter predictably harsh? What evidence of old Celtic ways remain in this tiny place that had so influenced my religious heritage?

Before visiting, I recalled that Iona had been a stepping stone in renewing the vitality of Christianity in northeastern England. If I went there, I could search for evidence of seventh-century hermit cells that housed a dispersed community of solitaries who came together periodically. I had heard that partial structures remain of a women's community from the thirteenth century, and for a men's order of the same period—the latter's buildings restored and now widely used for extended retreats during summer months. I had already been attracted to the music I had heard in America during the last few years from young people who visit the island in summer and bring back its rhythms and sounds. And, added to its other inducements, Iona is a small island—and I have a love for small islands I have never met! My formal preparations were two: a train ticket and written assurance that I would have a bed on arriving. But I had prepared myself in a number of ways, and was receptive to visiting a holy place.

⊗⊗

My fourth solitary pilgrimage is a pilgrimage of a different sort, a pilgrimage that has been underway for ten years: a journey into literature, poetic prose written long ago by people I can never meet but who lived in places I can still visit. At the center of my exploration is the person of Thomas Traherne, who spent much of his life in and near Hereford at the English-Welsh border. He lived from 1637 until 1674, a period of ferment and change that reshaped the country politically, socially, economically, and theologically. Appreciation of Traherne's artistic legacy has been slow in coming, largely because his writings were lost or misidentified for years. The unfolding drama is largely one of serendipity: a major manuscript discovered in London's bookstalls exactly a century ago, several works identified this century as his and not of other writers, and a dramatic recovery in the 1960s of yet another manuscript from a burning trash heap far from his home and three hundred years after his death.

I was first attracted to Thomas Traherne because his recollections of childhood echo my own experience of meeting God in nature. In a poem called "The Salutation" he writes, "He in our Childhood with us

Walks and with our Thoughts Mysteriously He talks."
Was I an early daydreamer—as adults reminded me
from time to time—or one invited into a mystery they
had since abandoned? Well into my adult years, long
before I was aware of Traherne, I was captured by the
profound realization that *all* of creation is intended for
my enjoyment—all for me, as indeed also for all other
people. I could enjoy the universe without needing to
possess any part of it. Yet I could not escape the
common human desire to "own" a tiny part of
creation—at the cost of a lessened valuing of the great
amount not personally possessed. How moved I was to
find a kindred soul in Traherne:

> You never enjoy the World aright, till the Sea itself
> floweth in your Veins, till you are clothed with the
> Heavens, and crowned with the Stars; and Perceiv
> yourself to be the Sole Heir of the whole World: and
> more then so, becaus Men are in it who are evry one
> Sole Heirs, as well as you. Till you can Sing and Rejoyce
> and Delight in God, as Misers do in Gold, and Kings in
> Scepters, you never enjoy the World.[1]

Where is my current pilgrimage leading? Recently I
visited the parish church in Credenhill where Traherne
had been rector, walked through the quadrangle of the
Oxford college where he studied, hiked through much
of the adjacent Wye Valley, and continued my reading of
Traherne's writings as well as the commentaries of
others. I view him as a gentle prophet who calls us to
treasure the earth and its creatures. In him I have found
a soul friend and a traveling companion, whatever shape
my journey takes.

---

1. *Centuries* 1.29, in Alan Bradford, ed., *Thomas Traherne: Selected
Poems and Prose* (London: Penguin Books, 1991).

Ultimately, this journey into literature is part of a larger solitary pilgrimage, one which must be termed lifelong. In the process of living, I have journeyed through a great deal of both familiar and new terrain—both geographic and mental. Personalizing themes enunciated by St. Paul, John Bunyan, and others, I see life itself as continuing pilgrimage: a quest born of deep longing and trust that my desire will be honored at the end of the seeking. But I resist the view that the hereafter is "real life," and that our existence here is primarily a journey to some celestial state. It is easy to mistake a mental image for the reality; the metaphor of journey informs life, but does not make life simply a journey. On the contrary, I find myself wanting to be present to more and more of the universe, not driven by anxiety that time is running out for me but longing to relate to a wider compass of creation. As Richard R. Niebuhr has noted:

> We are next to nothing if not kin to our globe and its atmosphere; but as we grow older we learn that we must employ our senses deliberately to keep this kinship alive. Yet, once we submit to this schooling, we seem not to be able to rest until we have invested ourselves in each of the world's elements: voyaged on its waters, climbed its mountains, breathed its high wind-streams, trekked over its hot sands.[2]

What am I most deeply seeking? Perhaps it is what Traherne called felicity. I am more inclined to label my quest as living in acknowledgment of the blessedness of life. Another word for it might be fulfillment, a word that Traherne would have used with reservation—as

---

2. Richard R. Niebuhr, "Pilgrims and Pioneers," in *Parabola* (August 1984), 6.

indeed he also freely believed in "heaven" as a gift to us in the present. But I must also admit that I want to live a holy life—which begins with my yearning for a whole life, as undivided and integrated as I can help it to be.

೦ஓ

My joyful response to pilgrim inquiry sustains my ongoing quest. An increasingly strong kinship with the world evokes feelings in me of wonder, reverence, and awe. Those particular feelings suggest to me that the quest includes spiritual dimensions that significantly shape my treatment of all members of the created world. G. K. Chesterton sagely noted that what the world needs are not more wonders but more wonder. Victor and Edith Turner, after years of studying the anthropology of pilgrimage, commented that if mysticism is interiorized pilgrimage, pilgrimage is exteriorized mysticism.[3] My brief rendering of these sentiments is that a guiding theology needs to accompany me on pilgrimage. A helpful beginning is to allow childlike wonder in my encounters, to invite God on my trips as well as on life's "journey," and to trust that God's story and mine intersect in both everyday and extraordinary ways.

Does the pilgrim longing arise from within, in response to an innate desire to move, or are we called forth in some way? "Perhaps rather than choosing," one commentator writes, "the pilgrim is chosen by his own way of being. For him what is important, finally, is to be in motion... [saying] with Don Juan: 'For me there is

3. Victor Turner and Edith Turner, *Image and Pilgrimage in Christian Culture* (New York: Columbia University Press, 1978), 7.

only the traveling on paths that have heart; there I travel, looking, looking, breathlessly.'"[4]

꩜

Questions for Reflection

Recall a trip on which you were among others, yet felt alone. How much of that feeling came from the actions of others, and how much from you?

Recall another journey that you chose to undertake alone, but further into the journey wished for companionship. What did you do to meet that need?

Have you experienced a journey that in hindsight reflects Robert Frost's words, "I took [the way] less traveled, and that has made all the difference." What made that journey a moment of decision and choice?

Recollect the first time you visited a place where immediately upon arrival you felt as if you were "coming home." What made it feel like home to you?

How likely are you to plan a proposed journey well in advance? Are you usually willing to yield parts of a carefully devised pilgrimage plan in order to take an

---

4. D. M. Dooling, "Focus," in *Parabola* (August 1984), 3.

alternate route? What would make a change in plans worthwhile to you?

Do you agree or disagree with D. M. Dooling's comment that "rather than choosing, the pilgrim is chosen by his own way of being"? Do you agree that "what is important, finally, is to be in motion"? How has that been true in your life?

ಠಂ

Appendix

Checklists for Planning Your Pilgrimage

The LORD answer you in the day of trouble
   the Name of the God of Jacob defend you;
Grant you your heart's desire
   and prosper all your plans.

Psalm 20:1 ,4 (BCP)

S ome form of planning is essential to any pilgrimage, no matter how unscheduled you want your trip to be. The following checklists have been helpful to me as I have planned pilgrimages for myself and for groups. I strongly recommend that you write down your responses, so that all practical issues can be covered and your anticipation will increase in the process.

The first, "Sightseeing or Pilgrimage?", will help you identify what sort of trip you are choosing to take, and what elements of pilgrimage might already be present.

The second, "My Proposed Journey," is a guide for shaping the travel and preparing oneself for the pilgrimage. Some details are important and are not to be missed: the whats, whens, and wheres of the journey.

The final list of questions, "Reflections on Each Stage of the Pilgrimage," can help guide you in the

131

more reflective side of your planning for pilgrimage. It will help you to chart your impressions upon approaching each new pilgrimage site and record your feelings about a final farewell before returning home. It may also reveal to you other personal changes that took place during your travel: the movement from initial apprehension to comfort, an unexpected bonding with certain places, or the sense of an important turning point in your life.

ༀ

Sightseeing or Pilgrimage?

1. Am I on a *quest,* searching for something in particular?
   How long have I been aware of my longing to do this? How do I experience this longing? What do I hope will be the outcome of this pilgrimage?

2. Do the pilgrimage *sites* to be visited inspire me?
   What features of the setting attract me most? Does the focus of the places to visit fit my needs?

3. What kind of *travel* will my pilgrimage require?
   How can I begin my journey without feeling rushed? What will encourage my receptivity and minimize my fatigue?

4. What *plans* do I need to make?
   How far ahead do I need to start my planning? How can I make my planning part of the anticipation of

my pilgrimage? How much will I plan ahead for my return? Have I taken the time to write my plans down in terms of what, when, and where?

5. Is this the right *time* for a pilgrimage?
Can I allow sufficient time for a pilgrimage? Does the journey seem timely for me? What rhythm of traveling and rest do I want to observe in my pilgrimage?

6. What *interaction*—if any—do I want with fellow pilgrims and others?
Should I choose a group or a solitary pilgrimage? If I travel as part of a group, how will I find time apart for myself each day? Am I prepared for very busy tourist crowds, or do I want a pilgrimage to solitary places?

7. Do I see myself as a *pilgrim?*
What safeguards can I make to support that perspective? Does it matter to me whether I am on pilgrimage or on a trip? What can I do differently to make this a pilgrimage, rather than simply a pleasure trip?

8. How do I best express *reverence* for the sacredness of the site?
How can I prepare myself spiritually? How can I remain silent and reflective amidst much activity?

∂⊘

My Proposed Journey

∂⊘ *What*

1. What do I want to *do* while on pilgrimage?

2. What *major outcome* of the journey am I hoping for? What will at least partially satisfy my longing? What will make the pilgrimage "worthwhile"?

3. What *theme or focus* do I want to choose that will help my pilgrimage be more than wandering?

4. What are the *essential details* of my plan, elements that I do not want to omit or forget?

∂⊘ *Where*

1. Where do I want to go while on pilgrimage? What are the *principal places* I hope to visit? What are the *secondary places* that would be nice to see if I have the time?

2. What *resources* can I seek out to inform my planning?

☙ *When*

1. What *calendar dates* would work for my pilgrimage?

2. What dates of *special events* or anniversaries are important to my pilgrimage? Are the sites accessible at those times?

☙ *Who*

1. Will I have *companions* during part or all of the pilgrimage? Who will they be?

2. With whom can I *share details* before my departure?

3. Whom could I *meet at various points* during my journey?

4. Who might be available for *sharing at intermediate points* on the journey?

5. Who will be my *contacts at home* during my absence?

ഔ *How*

1. What will be my primary *means of travel?*

2. How can I expect to *fund* my journey, including travel, food, admission, and lodging costs?

3. How I can make the journey a *reflective experience?* How can I incorporate regular meditation, journaling, art sketches, meeting with a mentor, regular prayer, or other reflective aids?

ഔ *Why*

1. Once again, *why am I undertaking the journey?* (Consider this question over a period of weeks before the journey, and write a short response each week.)

ഔ *Recording the Plan*

1. In what order do the various details of my journey need to be planned in advance?

2. What calendar dates can be reserved and planned in advance?

3. How do I plan to keep records en route of my reflections and experiences of the journey?

ठळ

Reflections on Each Stage of the Pilgrimage

ठळ *Preparation:*
 prior to leave-taking

1. How did it feel to tie up "loose ends" at home?

2. Did I have all that I needed to take with me ready to pack, or did I have to scramble at the last minute?

3. What objects or actions signified for me the importance of the upcoming adventure (choice of clothing, notebook, novel, prayer, a bon voyage party)?

ठळ *Impressions:*
 soon after leaving home

1. What is it like to be underway?

2. How does it feel to release all thoughts of home and routines?

୭୯ *Impressions:*
 after visiting each major site

1. What first impressions and feelings did I have as I approached this site?

2. How did this site relate to the other sites I have visited during this pilgrimage?

3. In what ways did I see myself as a pilgrim at this site?

4. What distracted me from my sense of pilgrimage at this site?

5. What specific sense impressions did I have at this site: sight, sound, touch, smell, taste, temperature, air movement, ease of movement, breathing?

6. Was I able to be silent and aware at this site?

7. What did I sense the site was trying to inform me about itself?

8. What did this site help me to discover about myself?

ᏸᏋ Departure:
just prior to returning home

1. Are there any momentoes I want to take home with me?

2. How and to whom do I need to say good-bye?

3. How do I feel about returning home?

ᏸᏋ Return:
en route home

1. What were the five high points of my time away? What made them high points for me?

2. What are five things I am thankful for on returning home?

Cowley Publications is a ministry of the Society of St. John the Evangelist, a religious community for men in the Episcopal Church. Emerging from the Society's tradition of prayer, theological reflection, and diversity of mission, the press is centered in the rich heritage of the Anglican Communion.

Cowley Publications seeks to provide books, audio cassettes, and other resources for the ongoing theological exploration and spiritual development of the Episcopal Church and others in the body of Christ. To this end, it is dedicated to developing a new generation of theological writers, encouraging them to produce timely, creative, and stimulating publications of excellence, and making these publications available widely, reaching both clergy and lay persons.